ETpedia™
Materials Writing

500 ideas
for creating
English language
materials

G
R
N
S M J P
F A Z B
Q X O T

Lindsay Clandfield and John Hughes

Series editor: John Hughes

www.myetpedia.com

ENGLISH TEACHING *professional*

ETpedia
Materials Writing

Published by:
Pavilion Publishing and Media Ltd
Rayford House
School Road
Hove BN3 5HX
UK
Tel: 01273 434 943
Fax: 01273 227 308

First published 2017

ISBN: 978-1-911028-62-8

PDF ebook ISBN: 978-1-911028-63-5

Epub ISBN: 978-1-911028-64-2

Kindle ISBN: 978-1-911028-65-9

Authors: Lindsay Clandfield and John Hughes

Editor: Helena Gomm

Production editor: Mike Benge, Pavilion Publishing and Media

Cover design: Emma Dawe, Pavilion Publishing and Media

Page layout and typesetting: Phil Morash, Pavilion Publishing and Media

Printing: Ashford Press

Contents

Writing complete lessons and worksheets

Writing supplementary materials

Writing materials for other teachers

Developing your materials writing skills

Introduction

10 reasons for using this resource

1. Supporting day-to-day materials writing

All English language teachers need to create their own materials at some stage in their working lives. Sometimes it's a quick gap-fill exercise to check if the students remember what they did in the previous lesson, or it might be an end-of-term test. Teachers write worksheets to go with videos and songs, and some even write whole sets of materials for use during the term by all the teachers in a school. Or perhaps they want to write and publish their own materials to share with the rest of the ELT world.

Given the vast range of materials that ELT teachers produce daily, it's perhaps surprising that there is so little support and guidance in the form of books and online resources. We hope that this book in the ETpedia series of teacher resources will provide that support.

2. From basic principles to extensive materials writing

This resource contains 50 units, covering everything an ELT teacher needs to know about getting started with writing materials – from the basics of creating sentence-level exercises to ways of exploiting longer texts, creating entire worksheets and producing whole sets of lesson materials.

3. Units of 10

Each unit contains 10 points. These can take the form of tips, ideas, examples of question types or checklists of general guidelines. Why 10? Because we believe that a list of 10 provides enough information both to inspire you and encourage you to develop your skills further.

4. New teachers

If you are just starting out in English language teaching, you may not have the confidence to produce large amounts of your own material, and you may be teaching from a coursebook or materials provided by more experienced colleagues. However, you may still encounter occasions when you wish to try out your own ideas or produce some material to supplement your coursebook. You will find lots of ideas here to help you and provide you with the building blocks to start creating (and later sharing) your own classroom and self-study materials.

5. Experienced teachers

If you have been teaching for a while, this resource may both remind you of the techniques needed for materials writing and also give you some fresh ideas for developing your materials writing skills.

6. Studying for an ELT qualification

Perhaps you are planning to take the Teaching Knowledge Test (TKT), or studying for another teaching qualification, such as a CELTA or Cert TESOL. On these kinds of courses, you will need to demonstrate your ability to create some basic materials, such as grammar or vocabulary exercises. For teachers taking higher-level qualifications, such as the DELTA, Diploma in TESOL or even an MA with a component in materials design and development, this book will be an invaluable reference.

7. Published ELT materials writers

For people who already have their materials published and who earn money from writing, this resource offers a useful set of checklists which you can turn to when you're in need of a few extra ideas or looking for a quick alternative way to design an exercise. It will help to remind you of the key points that you need to bear in mind when starting out on a new writing project. In addition, you may want to create your own set of tips to refer to, using the 'Write your own tips' pages at the end of the book.

8. Teacher trainers

If you are a teacher trainer, senior teacher or director of studies who delivers staff training on a range of topics, then the ideas that this resource offers could form the basis for sessions related to materials writing. You could choose one or two lists of tips from a particular section as the focus for a single training session.

9. Additional photocopiables and quotes

At the end of this book, you will find an Appendix with additional photocopiable materials. These can be used as they are or adapted and developed to suit your own context. Throughout the book you will also find quotes from experienced writers, sharing their views, ideas and experiences on producing ELT materials.

10. More time

If you are familiar with the other ETpedia resource books, you'll know that the books aim to save you time. The one thing that all teachers (and full-time materials writers) say that they lack is time. We hope that by sharing this collection of ideas, based on our many years of experience of writing for our own classes and, later, as published authors, we can save you time when it comes to producing your own materials.

"I'm a big fan of the ETpedia books as they offer a wealth of information. They are very easy to dip into as a reference as they are clearly labelled and divided into different categories. Perfect for novice teachers finding their feet in the world of EFL, experienced teachers who need a quick refresher on a certain subject or even for teacher trainers to use during input sessions. All in all, the ETpedia books have quickly become an EFL teacher's best companion!"

Glenn Standish, Director of Studies, International House, Toruń, Poland

10 ways to use this resource

This resource has been written for teachers who are writing materials to use with their own students, materials to be shared with and used by colleagues, or materials to be published online or in print. It can be read and used in different ways according to your needs, interests and level of experience.

1. Cover to cover

If you are new to the area of materials writing, you might be using this resource as an introductory text to the subject. If so, it's worth reading the book from cover to cover in order to get a thorough overview and grounding in how to write materials for English language learners and teachers.

2. Read a section

The contents page will direct you to different sections with groups of units. Some sections might not be immediately relevant to the type of materials you are working on, so ignore them for now. Other sections will be of instant relevance and will provide you with the key information you are looking for.

3. Go to the unit

If you are worried that your materials always follow the same patterns or use the same types of exercises, then go straight to the relevant unit and find nine other ways to structure your material.

4. Materials writer's block

You might be familiar with the term 'writer's block' in relation to novelists. However, there are also times when ELT materials writers simply cannot come up with the ideas they need. By dipping into the right section or unit, you should find the inspiration you're looking for.

5. Ability to evaluate materials

By learning the basics of materials planning and construction from this book, you will be better able to analyse published texts and decide whether they are suitable for your classes.

6. Supplement your coursebook

Many teachers find that they need to offer their students more practice than is found in their coursebook, or that the coursebook material needs to be adapted to suit their students' needs. You will find plenty of ideas in this book to help you write good supplementary exercises and to help you adapt existing exercises to make them more appropriate for your classes.

7. Develop new aspects of materials writing

If you have written worksheets or materials to be printed out and distributed to students, you might want to start thinking about developing other skills, such as writing for online materials. Take a look at Units 45 and 49 for this.

Introduction

8. Writing for other teachers

You may want to share the materials that you have written for your students with other teachers in your institution. In this case, you will need to produce teaching notes and answer keys to accompany your materials. See Units 41–43 for more information on how to write for teachers.

9. Develop your skills

If you are at the stage where you feel you are ready for a greater challenge – perhaps to share your materials with the wider world and get them published – read the final section. This looks at ways to develop your skills and prepare your work for publication. There are also suggestions on how to set about getting published.

10. Write your own 10

ELT materials writing is constantly evolving, particularly in the area of online materials. As you explore deeper into the subject and expand your own skills, you are bound to come up with your own ideas and find aspects of materials writing for which you would like to make your own list of 10 tips. Add your ideas to page 183 and share them with colleagues who are also writing their own materials. You could even share them with the whole world by visiting www.myetpedia.com where we regularly post lists of '10 ways' from people who use the ETpedia books. Visit the website for information on sharing your ideas.

"I frequently use the ideas in ETpedia as a kind of checklist when preparing my lessons."

Mario Lecluyze, teacher and teacher trainer, Belgium

Introduction

10 facts about the authors

Lindsay Clandfield ...

▶ got his first piece of material published in 1999 in iTs Magazine, a Barcelona-based magazine for teachers. The magazine wasn't taking submissions, but he banged on the door in person several times with various worksheets until they gave him a chance.

▶ has written books for teachers, including *Teaching Online and Dealing with Difficulties*, published by Delta Publishing. His latest book is *Interaction Online*, written with Jill Hadfield for the Cambridge Handbooks series. He has also written coursebook material for OUP and Macmillan, and was the lead author for the adult course *Global*.

▶ has won several awards for writing, including the Ben Warren Award and two English Speaking Union awards, both of which earned him visits to Buckingham Palace.

▶ started an e-publishing venture called The Round (with Luke Meddings), in which authors self-publish e-books within a collective framework. More than 25 books have been published there and are available at www.the-round.com

▶ has experimented with all different kinds of content creation, from writing for blogs to podcasting to writing for apps. His most unusual writing was a series of books called *Extreme Language Teaching*, which included *English for the Zombie Apocalypse* and *English for the Alien Invasion*.

▶ can be found at www.lindsayclandfield.com, where he can be contacted for teacher training or conferences and where you can find all his writing.

John Hughes ...

▶ remembers writing his first ELT material in 1992 on a course preparing him to teach for the first time. The worksheet was a set of job adverts adapted from a newspaper, and the students had to find key vocabulary and then practise interviewing each other.

▶ was first published in magazines such as *English Teaching Professional* and *Modern English Teacher*. He had a regular advice column for ELT teachers in *The Guardian Weekly* for a number of years.

▶ published his first teacher's book in 2002 and is the author and co-author of classroom and self-study materials including *Business Result*, *Business Focus*, *Successful Meetings and Presentations*, *Oxford EAP A2 (Oxford)*, *Life*, *Practical Grammar*, *Spotlight on FCE*, *Success with BEC Vantage*, *Total Business 2*, *Aspire* (National Geographic Learning) and *Telephone English* (Macmillan).

▶ runs training courses in ELT materials writing and offers consultancy in developing in-house materials to language schools and organisations.

▶ wrote the very first ETpedia title for Pavilion Publishing. He is the series editor for ETpedia resource titles. In 2016, with co-author Robert McLarty, his book *ETpedia Business English* won The David Riley Award for Innovation in Business English and ESP.

Thanks and acknowledgements

The authors would like to thank Helena Gomm, Emma Grisewood, the team at Pavilion Publishing, and all the English teachers and materials writers who shared their thoughts and expertise.

Writing materials for the first time

This introductory section begins by looking at why teachers need to write their own materials. If you are trying to write your own materials for the first time, a useful first step is to think about your reasons for doing so and to consider some of the ways in which you can get started.

Unit 1 gives 10 reasons why teachers might choose to write their own materials. Do any of these apply to you? Do you have a reason that isn't listed here?

Unit 2 gives you a checklist of skills and qualities to consider. If you have been teaching and writing your own materials for a while, you will most likely possess some of these skills already, but you should also find a fresh perspective on what characterises an effective writer. This unit will also give you food for thought on areas that you might like to develop while using this resource.

Units 3 and 4 make sure you are familiar with the key terms needed to talk about materials writing and the types of materials commonly produced by teachers around the world. We make use of the terms presented in these two units throughout this book, so even if you have plenty of materials writing experience, it's worth reviewing these key terms and concepts.

10 reasons why English language teachers start writing materials

All English lessons have a teacher and at least one student. These two elements are at the core of any class, but there is also a third element: the materials that teacher and student(s) might need to use at certain stages of the lesson. These might include reading texts, photographs with questions, flashcards, gap-fill exercises, etc. Teaching materials may take the form of worksheets, coursebooks (printed or, increasingly, on-screen), videos and audio recordings. However, even with a whole library and collection of published materials at their disposal, there are times when teachers need to create and write their own materials. Here are 10 reasons why.

1. To test the students' progress

When we think of materials writing, we usually picture nicely designed worksheets for a complete lesson or a set of self-study exercises. In fact, the first type of material that many teachers write is a test. Typically, we'll write tests that check our students' progress after a few weeks, or perhaps an end-of-term test. It's rare to find a ready-made test that covers exactly what you have taught over the course of a term, so it is often necessary to create you own.

2. You don't have course materials or a coursebook

There's a very pragmatic reason why you may need to write your own materials: that's if you don't have a set of course materials or a coursebook to follow. In this situation, it's worth teaming up with other teachers who teach the same course and working together to build up a bank of materials that everyone can make use of.

3. The coursebook doesn't cover the whole syllabus

Even if you do have access to materials or a coursebook to follow, you may still find that it doesn't cover everything you need to suit your teaching context. In this case, you'll need to create supplementary materials, such as extra readings or extra listenings to use in class, or extra exercises to set for homework.

4. To teach specific language

You may find that you have to write original materials when working with students who need English for specific purposes. For example, if you have a group of engineers, it's unlikely that you will find published materials which meet their exact requirements in terms of language. In this situation, it is often a good idea to use texts from the students' own fields, and turn them into classroom materials. For example, you might create exercises based around a technical document.

5. To provide material for personal interest

Whilst published material aims to include topics and themes which will be of interest to a large number of students, it can never quite match up to a well-chosen text which has been selected because you know your students' personal tastes and interests. Perhaps you have a class of teenagers who are currently listening to a particular type of music, so you might incorporate the song lyrics into a lesson. Or maybe you find a reading text in a magazine which is about the town or region that your students come from. Materials that draw on personal interest can often really motivate your class in a way that other material may not.

Unit 1

6. When students bring something they want to use in class

Following on from reason 5 above, you sometimes find that students bring something in English to class to show you. With younger students, this could be a video of a film in English that they want help understanding; with adult students, it may be a piece of correspondence in English that they have received at work. This situation offers you an opportunity to adapt such texts into classroom materials.

7. To create online material

As more and more schools offer their students online materials, either as an additional resource or as a complete replacement for paper-based lessons, many teacher-writers are involved in converting existing paper materials to online formats or originating completely new online material. Learning platforms such as Moodle require teachers to learn how to use technology for creative online activities, but at the heart of the process remains the ability to produce good materials for language teaching in the form of reading and listening texts, and exercises that practise grammar, vocabulary, pronunciation, and so on.

8. It's in the job description

Materials writing is simply part of that long list of skills that teachers must have. It might be something as basic as creating and writing a short grammar presentation which you put up on your board to help teach a language point. Or it can be finding a news article which you think your students might be interested in reading and so you write some comprehension questions to check their understanding. Even before you enter the classroom as a paid professional, you will find that many teacher training courses include a component on making your own classroom materials and trying them out in your first lessons.

9. It's fun!

For many teachers, writing materials is one of the best parts of being a teacher because it can be creative and so it's fun to do. It allows you to use your imagination and to experiment with ideas. Once you start making your own materials, there's no going back!

10. For professional development and beyond

Finally, you can also regard materials writing as a form of professional development with which you can improve your skill set. The more you write, the more you increase your chances of getting further opportunities to write. For example, you may be asked to produce a set of tests for your whole school, a bank of materials for specialist courses, or even a complete book or online course which is published and sold.

"We all start writing our own stuff because we want to provide interesting content and activities for our students – content and activities which we really want to use. We do it because it feels great and makes us better teachers!"

Jeremy Harmer, writer, presenter, teacher and trainer

Unit 1

10 skills and qualities of an ELT materials writer

Professional material writing requires certain skills and qualities. Below are 10 of them. At this stage, don't worry if you don't think you possess all these characteristics! The more you try writing your own materials, the more you will develop these skills and qualities over time.

1. Teaching skills

We can assume that everyone who reads this book is either training to be a teacher, is already a teacher with experience of different types of learners, or is someone who has taught and now works in other areas, such as educational management or teacher training. Whatever your current background, the fact that you have taught means that you have the most basic job requirement when it comes to writing materials.

2. English language skills

You need a good knowledge of English, so that you are able to write materials which can teach students different language points; for example, if you need to write material that presents the rules for the past simple, accompanied by exercises that practise the tense, then obviously you need to have a confident grasp of its form, meaning and use. In addition to that, it's necessary either to have or to develop an ability to write in a style of English which students will understand and that teachers will find easy to follow.

3. An interest in other materials

People who write their own classroom materials generally have an interest in and wide-ranging knowledge of published materials. Teaching from a variety of coursebooks or worksheets means you have probably developed your own sense of what works well and what doesn't work in different classroom settings. This will help to influence your own materials writing.

4. The ability to understand student interests and needs

All effective materials come from knowing what it is that interests your students. Write for the needs of the students; so if they are teenagers, they might want to read texts about popular culture. If the materials are for people who need English for work, then use the kinds of contexts they work in or language that they need as your starting point.

5. Empathy with teachers

You might only write materials for your own lessons at first, but it's often the case that teachers who like writing start sharing materials with other teachers. In this situation, material writers are in the position of trying to make their fellow teachers' working lives easier. Teachers work long hours and are always short of time, so one important job is to provide teachers with materials that reduce their preparation time. Because of this, good materials writers need to make their materials as teacher-friendly as possible.

6. Keyboard skills

It's true that you can still make classroom materials by writing by hand and sticking and gluing pictures. However, nowadays, most classroom materials are created on screens and printed out or put online. Materials writers need a competent level of computer keyboard skills. Primarily, they use word processing programs because they need to write and edit language exercises. They also need the ability to insert images, create tables and add basic design features to the document. Internet skills and the ability to use search engines are also part of a materials writer's skill set.

7. Risk-taking

Materials writers are often teachers who take risks. When we write our own materials, we put a little of ourselves into them. We take a risk that the material might not work properly for some reason or that our students might not enjoy using them. When we lend a worksheet we have made to a colleague, there's the danger that they might not like what we've written. In other words, materials writers have to be prepared to take a risk, trust their own instincts, and not be daunted or discouraged if it doesn't work first time.

8. Reflective

Writing is a process. We often write a first draft, then a second and a third. With materials writing, part of the process is to write something, then teach with it, then rewrite it, then teach with it again until we feel it's working. And of course, materials sometimes have to be rewritten or adapted for different students. So as we are 'risk-takers' in 7, we also have to be willing to make mistakes, and reflect on them.

9. Ability to self-edit

As teachers, we often start to have 'favourite lessons'. These are lessons that we've done with many classes and they always seem to 'work'. Similarly, when we write materials, we sometimes have an attachment to certain worksheets or exercise types that we feel work very well; and in certain contexts, perhaps they do. But it can also happen that material we think works well does not work so well (or at all) for other teachers or in other classroom situations. Also, materials can become out-of-date if, for example, they are based on a specific news text that has lost current relevance or song lyrics that were popular in the teacher's youth but of no interest to the current generation of students. In other words, we need the ability to self-edit so that we rewrite if necessary or even stop pursuing an idea that seems good but in classroom terms does not work.

10. A 'materials radar'

Over time, experienced ELT materials writers tend to develop what can be described as their 'radar' or second sense for what might come in useful in the future. They often collect images, leaflets, newspaper articles, links and any kind of stimuli or inspiration that they can use in their materials. For example, you might see a busker in the street and take a photograph for use in a lesson on the topic of performance. Or while reading the newspaper, you come across a 'day-in-the-life' type interview with a famous celebrity. Often this type of text includes use of the present simple so you save the article for a reading lesson you have in mind. And perhaps one of your students shows you a funny online video which you want to turn into the basis for a video worksheet. Once you start materials writing on a regular basis, you'll find it hard to turn your 'materials radar' off, as you'll always be on the lookout for good ideas.

10 key terms and categories in ELT materials writing

Like any profession, the world of ELT has its own terminology or 'jargon'. Materials writing also tends to use certain terms. You are probably familiar with many of them already, but here are 10 key terms which are useful when talking about materials writing and which appear, therefore, throughout this book. (Also see Unit 45 on key terms related to digital materials writing.)

1. In-class or classroom materials

Any materials that are specially written for use with students in the classroom or during a lesson (also online) can be referred to as 'in-class'. Unlike other materials, they are written with the assumption that a teacher is present to work with the students. This affects the assumptions you make about the materials. For example, you might write the material so that some of the decision-making is left in the hands of the teacher (eg whether the students work in pairs, groups or on their own to complete a task). Also, as well as including exercises and tasks with single right/wrong answers, in-class materials can include more open-ended tasks, such as discussion questions, role plays and exercises where the students have to give a personal response, because the teacher is available to manage the outcomes. Typically, a published student's book is an example of in-class or classroom material.

2. Self-study materials

These materials generally include lots of single right/wrong type exercises; so you'll find plenty of gap-fill exercises and multiple-choice questions. They are written so that a student can work through them alone and doesn't need external help. As well as exercises, self-study material might include some kind of language reference section (see the next item) to provide additional help. With self-study materials, the writer only has the student in mind and must write accordingly. In publishing, self-study materials are written as both printed workbooks and as online material, which students work through on screen.

3. Language reference

Language reference material refers to anything that sets out to explain a language point. You will often find such material at the end of a coursebook, where the students can refer to it in order to check their understanding of a grammar point. With online courses, the students can often click to read a pop-up box containing information about grammar or vocabulary. (See Unit 40.)

4. Teacher's notes

When you first write materials for your own lessons, you probably don't need teacher's notes because you already know how to use the material. But once you start sharing your material, and even publishing it, other teachers will need notes. As a minimum, these will include an answer key, but teachers will also want ideas on how they can adapt the materials according to their own circumstances. Publishers provide teacher's books with sets of course materials, and these are typical of what you'd expect from a set of teacher's notes. (See Unit 41.)

Unit 3

5. Worksheets

'Worksheet' is a general term, usually referring to one or two A4-sized pieces of paper with a series of exercises. A worksheet can often form the basis for a whole in-class lesson or may be something that the teacher provides for the students to complete as homework. We can also be more specific and talk about 'song worksheets' or 'reading worksheets'. These might have a set of song lyrics with some accompanying exercises or a text from a newspaper and some comprehension questions.

6. Photocopiable resources

Photocopiable resources are usually extra materials that are either provided at the back of a teacher's book or can be printed as a pdf from a website. They are often photocopiable worksheets (see above) that accompany a set of coursebooks or form a collection of course materials for use by a group of teachers. They are formatted in such a way as to make them easy to photocopy – and if they are published as photocopiable, the copyright holder is giving permission for them to be copied. Photocopiable resources tend to include free practice or game-like activities. (See Appendix, pages 170–182.)

7. Tests

A test is an exercise or set of exercises designed to find out how much the students know. The purpose may be to determine which class they should go in, to assess the progress they are making, to find out how much they have learnt at the end of a course, etc. High-stakes tests may give the students a qualification which will affect their future careers. Teachers often write their own tests for a variety of reasons. These include making sure that the test contains material that the teacher has taught the students that semester or year (and only that material). The contents of any test need to reflect the content of the course and the exercise types that the students are already familiar with. The need for tests to be tailor-made in this way means that they are amongst the materials most commonly written by teachers.

8. Digital and online material

More and more teaching and testing material is now digital, rather than paper-based. Students access it online, often through virtual learning environments such as Moodle. The content is often similar to that used in self-study materials or tests, as each student will generally be working alone on a computer to complete the tasks. Although the exercises may be similar to those in paper-based materials, the digital world offers both constraints and enhancement. The exercise types that are available to writers of digital material are constrained by what the particular software being used can offer. As a result, they are often limited to multiple-choice and gap-fill. However, technological advances are now offering automatic marking and feedback as well as adaptive materials where the computer reacts to the students' answers by offering either more challenging or less challenging tasks as appropriate. Writing digital materials generally means working with a template or learning platform and means that the writer may have to develop a new set of skills.

Unit 3

9. Audio and video

Whilst video and sound recording have been possible for decades, the increase in the ownership of smartphones with built-in recording and videoing facilities and the development of online video editing tools have meant that it has never been easier for teachers to write and record their own audio and video sequences both in and outside the classroom. This could mean anything from interviewing someone and writing comprehension questions based on the interview, to writing the script for a mini-drama, filming it with students or friends and writing a worksheet to go with it. In many ways, creating audio and video for language learning is one of the most exciting areas in materials writing at the moment because there is so much potential for experimentation and creativity. Many online learning websites offer podcast listenings, and most major ELT publishers now include video components as part of a complete course package. This growth area in ELT simply reflects the strength of audio and video in the students' lives, so materials writing in the future will definitely require us to develop our scriptwriting skills. (See Units 21 and 22.)

10. Methodology resources

One final strand of materials writing is writing about language teaching. For example, you might write an article on the key points of motivating students, or how to approach teaching collocation. Many magazines and journals such as *English Teaching Professional* and *Modern English Teacher* publish articles on a whole range of topics – and these are all written by practising teachers. There are also publishers' websites and blogs which commission posts on different topics related to ELT methodology. Some Teacher's guides that accompany coursebooks also have short sections on different aspects of methodology. Clearly, writing this kind of material is very different from writing in-class or self-study materials for students, but it is a form of writing that can be very satisfying for teachers who have something to say and want to see their ideas in print. (See Unit 50.)

"When you are writing materials for your classes, the most important aspect is being able to target your audience, in terms of context, age, language ability and interest. If you can do that creatively, even better!"

Vicky Saumell, EFL teacher trainer and materials writer, Buenos Aires, Argentina

Unit 3

10 types of language materials that teachers often start writing

It is common to find that teachers don't think of themselves as materials writers. Perhaps they perceive the 'materials writer' only in terms of the published author, producing a series of coursebooks, and the idea of 'materials writing' sounds much too challenging. In reality, however, almost all language teachers start writing materials, because it's part of what teaching is. The moment you open a new document on your computer, or take a blank piece of paper and pen, and you begin writing something that will be read by your students, you are creating materials. Indeed, we have found that many teachers consider creating their own materials as part of their professional development. The amount and scope of the materials you write may vary, from a simple exercise to an entire course. Let's look at the typical types of language materials that teachers write.

1. An exercise

By far the most common thing that teachers start writing is a language practice exercise. This is often based around a simple exercise format, such as eight gap-fill questions or a set of comprehension questions based on a text. Typically, it supplements something in the coursebook or the course syllabus and provides extra practice. The most common kinds of exercises are grammar and/or vocabulary exercises. (See Units 6–7.)

2. An informal test

Although most current coursebooks come with a whole battery of tests that the teacher can use, many teachers still like to (or need to) create their own informal tests so that they can include topics or language that came up in class but wasn't covered in the book. These could be short language tests for use in class, or tests that the students complete at home. (See Unit 39.)

3. Reading material

After writing short exercises and tests, many teachers like to bring their own material on current topics and themes to the class. This can often take the form of a short text, taken from a news website or other internet source. The text may be slightly adapted or shortened if it's too hard, and is usually accompanied by comprehension questions, which the teacher writes. This is a great way to supplement your coursebook with something a bit more up-to-date and engaging. (See Units 17–19.)

4. A song worksheet

One very popular piece of material is a song worksheet, using the lyrics of a song and making them into some kind of exercise or exercises. And if you know that your students are currently listening to a particular song or artist, using that in class is a great way to motivate them. (See Unit 37.)

5. Games

One area of writing and creating materials that teachers often try early on is game-like activities. These could be simple board games with questions for the students to answer, cards for a game of bingo, or other more elaborate and complicated games to review and practise different language elements. Wordsearch games and crossword puzzles are two common favourites for language teachers. (See Units 34–35.)

Unit 4

6. Listening material

This is often a series of exercises or activities to accompany a listening that the teacher wants to use in class. The activities could be based around a 'live listening' (where the teacher will provide the audio material live in the form of a story or presentation), or they could be based around existing recorded audio (that the teacher wants to exploit further or differently from the way it is done in the coursebook). Sometimes teachers write activities for audio material that they have recorded themselves or that they have obtained elsewhere and which doesn't have any accompanying exercises. Note that one of the biggest challenges here is obtaining a good quality recording for use in class. (See Unit 20.)

7. Video material

This is similar to 6 above, except that material is based around an audiovisual text. Many teachers start out by creating worksheets which go with YouTube videos, such as TED talks. And more and more teachers are also starting to write and produce their own videos from scratch, using the range of video editing software freely available online. (See Unit 38.)

8. Speaking material

In their very first lesson of a new course, many teachers like to write and give the students a questionnaire which they can use with each other to find out more about their classmates. Writing a simple questionnaire is just one effective way of creating speaking material. You can also write role cards, outlining different situations for the students to role play, or 'information-gap' worksheets, where the students need to communicate with each other to find out missing information. Questions and statements for students to discuss or debate are also forms of speaking material which teachers can write. (See Units 23–24.)

9. Flashcards and other vocabulary teaching aids

Flashcards can have words, pictures or both pictures and words on them. While flashcards are the most common tools for presenting vocabulary, there are other kinds of materials that teachers produce to teach new words and phrases. These include mindmaps, wordlists and explanations. Some of these materials may be intended for the students' own reference. With access to the internet and large online image banks, it's easier than ever for teachers to make attractive material for teaching vocabulary.

10. Teacher's notes

If a teacher has written any of the above simply for his or her own class, then probably no teaching notes are required beyond an answer key. However, when you write material to be used by someone else, it's all too easy to assume that others will automatically understand how to use what you write. But this is very often not the case! Writing good teaching notes is very important when you begin to put your material into someone else's hands. You will need to consider how experienced they are and whether you need to spell out every step of the activity or not. Writing clear rubrics, warning teachers in advance what extra material they might need and what problems they might encounter with the material, also forms part of the teacher's notes. See Units 41–42 for more details on this.

Writing language exercises and different types of questions

The exercise and question types in this section are mainly suited to materials written for self study or for inclusion in classroom materials where a controlled practice stage is required. The different question types can also be used for writing tests and for development of online materials and content for learning platforms.

This section begins with ideas and advice for producing materials for presenting and practising new language. The first few units help you to plan and prepare materials for teaching grammar, vocabulary and pronunciation. Units 5 to 8 look at some common ways to introduce language, and Unit 9 looks at how to structure an entire exercise.

The second half of the section introduces a variety of question types that we often take for granted in the materials we use, but which take a considerable amount of thought and care to write effectively. Starting with the basic gap-fill sentence, moving on to the multiple-choice question and beyond, Units 10 to 16 are a compendium of different question types. They will give you the ideas you need to add variety and diversity to your exercises.

Once you have read this section and you start to write your own exercises and questions, always write answer keys as a form of quality control; even the smallest mistake when writing exercises can mislead a student.

10 ways to present new language

When we talk about new language, we usually mean grammar or vocabulary. If you are writing materials with a grammar or vocabulary focus, you'll need to begin with an exercise that presents the language. For vocabulary, the difference between presenting and practising in materials is often blurry (see Unit 7). For grammar, you typically have two choices when creating a presentation: either to teach the rule explicitly or to let the students discover it themselves by seeing the language in a natural context. In either case, the following tips will be helpful if you are presenting new language through a text. Tips 1 to 4 deal with presenting new language in context.

1. Find the right context

Think of a natural-sounding context for the grammar point or vocabulary area you want to present, and use that to create your sample sentences. A text about unusual journeys is a natural context for travel vocabulary, just as a text about a memorable trip is a natural context for the past simple. For several examples of different natural contexts for common grammar points see Appendix Unit 5.

2. Create examples that include the language

If you are using a text with examples of your target language in it, that's great. If not, you might want to write or adapt a text so that it includes some good examples. Note that this could be a reading text or a listening text, or it could be a dialogue that the students both read and listen to. Most modern materials try to contextualise the target language in this way and avoid presenting it in a vacuum. (Examples that do present grammar or vocabulary in this way are sometimes critically called 'decontextualised sentences').

3. Highlight or repeat examples from your text

You will want to draw your students' attention to the target language in the text. One way is to have lots and lots of examples of it (a process sometimes called 'input flooding'). Here is a text that is input flooding the present perfect with already:

It's 10am and Jeremy has already done a lot of housework. He has already swept the floors. He has already done the shopping. He has already made the beds. He has already cleaned the bathroom. He's very tired!

Alternatively, you can highlight the target language by putting it in bold or underlining it in the text, or by extracting key examples and repeating them to the students afterwards.

4. Don't push it

Sometimes new materials writers feel they have to include all the key vocabulary they want to teach in a text. Or they feel that there should be affirmative, negative and question forms for every new verb. Be aware that the more you force examples into the text, the more unnatural it will sound. In fact, sometimes a context you think is perfect for exemplifying a language point might not turn out to be very natural. Try reading your text with the target language aloud. Does it feel like you've put too much in? Does it sound awkward? If you answer yes to either of these questions, you need to re-examine the text.

5. Include the rule in the presentation

Here is an example of a rule:

We use the zero article with uncountable or plural nouns to talk about things in general.

The way you include a rule will depend on the approach you wish to take to grammar as a whole. If you give the rule above and ask the students to do an exercise which requires them to understand that rule, you are using a more deductive approach. An inductive approach means that the students do an exercise and then try to figure out the rule. It might be written like this:

Look at the examples of sentences with no article (zero article). Can you make a rule about when we use the zero article?

Sometimes you can provide support or help in formulating the rule (see tip 8).

Neither the inductive nor the deductive method is necessarily better, although it's more fashionable to teach grammar rules inductively these days.

6. Be concise

Some people find it difficult to write grammar rules. By trying to cover every aspect of a particular language point, they tend to make their explanations too long and complicated. It is better to be concise and to make your explanations as simple as possible. Here is an example of a simple grammar rule made more complicated.

You can show possession by adding an apostrophe and the letter 's' to a noun or noun phrase, for example: John's mother. This is called the Saxon genitive. In the case of plural nouns ending in -s, possession can be shown simply by adding an apostrophe at the end, for example: my parents' house.

This rule is too hard and complex for beginners. More simple would be something like this:

Use 's to show possession: John's mother.

If the word ends in an s, add ': My parents' house.

If you get stuck, a good idea is to have several grammar books on hand to look at how other authors have explained the same grammar point.

7. Use prescriptive language and descriptive language appropriately

We often use prescriptive language when we want to describe a fixed rule such as *Don't use to + infinitive after a modal verb.* However, depending on the context and the level of the students, sometimes we might have to describe a rule. Sometimes this will be a rule which has exceptions, but we need to give the students some guidelines. So we use descriptive language which makes use of phrases such as *usually*, *often* and *tends to*. For example, we might write *We don't usually use 'much' in affirmative sentences in modern English. We use 'a lot of' instead.*

8. Ask the students to complete the rule

This tip and the one that follows are more characteristic of an inductive approach than a deductive approach. Here you give a partial rule and ask the students to look at examples and try to complete it. For example: *To make most plurals in English, we add ____ to the noun.*

9. Give an example/examples and ask questions to get a rule

Here, you give examples and questions to guide the students to the rule. For example:

Look at the examples of 'be going to' in the text. Answer the questions.

What form of the verb comes after 'be going to'?

Do we use 'be going to' to talk about the past, present or future?

10. Give a task that will require use of the language

One approach to presenting a grammar or vocabulary point would be to start by asking the students to do a task that requires the target language, then to present an example of the completed task with the language in it, and then to teach the target language explicitly. For example, you might ask the students to speculate about what they would say if they met a famous person from history. Then you might play a listening or read a text with other people answering the same question. From this listening or reading, you extract examples of the second conditional and then teach the rules for forming it. This takes a more task-based approach to the material, and is sometimes called a test-teach-test approach.

"No single method of grammar presentation is going to be appropriate for all grammar items, nor for all learners, nor for all learning contexts."

Scott Thornbury, teacher educator and ELT author

Unit 5

10 types of grammar exercise

Once you have presented a grammar point, you'll need to set some practice exercises. Ideally, your exercises should involve practice of both the form and the meaning of the grammar point. When practising the form, make sure that you cover all the forms you are aiming at. For example, if your target grammar is the present simple affirmative, negative and question forms, then have a balance of each of those. Here are 10 types of task that teachers often use when writing controlled grammar practice exercises.

1. Gap-fill

Gap-fills are the most common and straightforward type of grammar exercise. For example, you can write an instruction and start the gap-fill like this:

Write the verbs in brackets in the past simple tense.

1. I _____ (go) for a long walk yesterday.

2. They _____ (leave) this house over a year ago.

3. He _____ (not/be) at work last week.

Answers: 1. went, 2. left, 3. wasn't

In general, gap-fills are fairly mechanical, but they certainly help to provide practice with form and help the teacher to check if the students know how to use a grammar item correctly. Note also that when the question is only one sentence and provides very little context, there is often a greater likelihood of multiple answers which might be correct in certain situations, so remember to write an answer key to check the exercise and look out for unintended answers.

For many more ways on using gap-fill exercises, see Units 10–11.

2. Multiple-choice

Multiple-choice questions (which are, in fact, a type of gap-fill) offer an alternative exercise. You could change the first question in the example exercise in 1, like this:

Choose the correct verb for the sentences.

1. I _____ for a long walk yesterday.

A go	B going	C went

Answers: 1.C

You can adjust the level of difficulty by increasing or decreasing the number of options, remembering that the more options you provide, the more time you will need to spend checking that only one option really fits correctly.

See Unit 12 for more about writing multiple-choice questions.

3. Complete a chart

Another way to check if the students know the form of a grammar item is to create a chart or table for them to fill in. The advantage of this is that once the students have filled it in, they can refer back to it later when they are trying to use the language productively. Here is an example for the past form of the verb 'to be'.

Complete the chart with the missing words.

	Affirmative	Negative	
I He/She/It	was 1._____	wasn't 2._____	on holiday.
We You They	were 3._____ 5._____	weren't 4._____ 6._____	on holiday.

Answers: 1. was, 2. wasn't, 3. were, 4. weren't, 5. were, 6. weren't

4. Create sentences from prompts

To make a more challenging grammar exercise, you can provide key words from a sentence separated with a backslash /. The students then need to make a sentence with the words, maybe adding other grammar words (such as auxiliaries). The example below is for forming questions about the past.

Make questions about last night. Then ask your partner.

you/watch/television?

you/make/dinner?

you/read/book?

Answers: Did you watch television last night? Did you make dinner? Did you read a book?

Unit 6

5. Rewrite sentences

This is a simple low-level exercise type that's useful with tenses, in particular. It's especially good for practising different forms.

Rewrite the sentences in the negative.

1. *Her name is Lorena.*

2. *She comes from Spain.*

3. *She works in Germany.*

Answers: 1. Her name isn't Lorena. 2. She doesn't come from Spain. 3. She doesn't work in Germany.

---

6. Correct or incorrect?

Write this exercise to check form and to target common mistakes that students make.

Decide if these sentences are correct ✔ or incorrect ✗.

1. *I sent some flowers to my mother.*

2. *We gave to the teacher a present.*

3. *Please say her it's my birthday party on Friday.*

Answers: 1. I sent some flowers to my mother. ✔ 2. We gave to the teacher a present. ✗
3. Please say her it's my birthday party on Friday. ✗

---

7. Contrasting sentences

At higher levels, when you are writing materials which address subtle differences in grammar usage, a good exercise is to have the students contrast pairs of sentences and talk about what they think the difference is. Alternatively, you can guide them towards guessing the difference with questions, like this:

Compare the pairs of sentences and answer the questions.

1. *My family lives in a small town in Brazil.*
2. *My family is living in a small town in Brazil.*

a) Which sentence describes a temporary situation?
b) Which sentence describes a permanent situation?

Answers: 1.b, 2.a

Unit 6

8. Underline examples of (target) grammar in the text

If you have used a reading text in class, you can analyse it for examples of a target grammar point. Your rubric might read: *Now read the text again and underline any verbs in the present perfect simple tense.*

This is a useful way to get the students to notice how grammar is used in context, and it can also be a useful way to introduce a grammar point into a skills-based lesson.

9. Translate sentences into your language

If you know that the materials you are writing will be used with monolingual classes where the teacher shares the students' L1, you could make effective use of translation. So the instruction on the page might be: *Translate the sentences into your language. How does the way in which these ideas are expressed in your language differ from the way they are expressed in English?*

10. Personalisation

When writing grammar exercises with in-class materials where the teacher can check what's written and discuss it with the students, adding exercises which require the students to personalise the grammar make it relevant and memorable. Here is an exercise you could write to practise adverbs of frequency and everyday verbs:

Rewrite the sentences below so they are true for you.

I always make the bed.

I hardly ever do the dishes.

Other exercise rubrics like this include:

> *Make the sentences true for your country.*
>
> *Change the sentences so they are about people you know.*

10 types of vocabulary exercise

Sometimes there is very little difference between an exercise that presents a new word and an exercise that practises it. Sometimes an exercise can do both. When writing materials, you will usually want to include practice for vocabulary items that are to become part of the learners' active vocabulary (as opposed to their passive vocabulary: the words and phrases they may know but don't actually use). Practice exercises will mostly focus on the meaning of vocabulary items, but may also practise spelling and collocation.

1. Word to a picture

Sometimes a good photo or illustration is the quickest way to teach a word or phrase. So you could write seven or eight words/phrases at the beginning of the exercise and then provide photos to match them to, like this:

Match these verb + noun collocations to the pictures.

1. hail a taxi   a)

2. board a plane   b)

3. catch a bus   c)

Answers: 1.c, 2.b, 3.a

---

2. Word to a definition

As with using pictures in 1., your exercise could ask the students to match the words to definitions. This type of exercise is normally used in higher-level materials.

Match these parts of a piece of clothing to a–c.

1. sleeve

a) the part of a piece of clothing around your neck

2. cuff

b) the part of a piece of clothing that covers your arm

3. collar

c) the part of a piece of clothing that goes round your wrist

Answers: 1.b, 2.c, 3.a

---

3. Jumbled letters

Once the students have done exercises which present the vocabulary, you can write this kind of exercise for practice of spelling.

Use these letters to make words connected with food.

| usop | ladas | team | shif | debar |

Answers: *soup, salad, meat, fish, bread*

---

4. Opposites

Some lexical sets come with obvious pairs of opposite words so this kind of exercise is useful.

Match the word to its opposite.

1. hot

a) damp

2. dry

b) cold

3. dark

c) light

Answers: 1.b, 2.a, 3.c

Unit 7

5. Odd word out

Exercises where the students choose the odd word out check their understanding of the relationship between different words. The rubric (see the example below) can also ask them to write why.

Decide which word is the odd word out? Write your reason(s).

1. seagull eagle pigeon squirrel dove

2. whale dolphin salmon eel spider

Answers: 1. squirrel, because it doesn't fly. 2. spider, because it doesn't live in the sea.

---

6. Word forms

You can use tables in your materials in a number of ways. One of the most effective is for word-building and focusing on different forms of words.

Complete the table with the correct form of the word.

Noun	Adjective
comfort	1.
2.	happy

Answers: 1. comfortable, 2. happiness

---

7. Categories

If you are writing material around a set of vocabulary which also has sub-groups of words within it (such as body parts, types of business, different foods, etc.), the following type of categorisation exercise is useful.

Put these words in the correct category.

back   thigh   lip   mouth   chest   knee

1. Head and face	2. Arm and leg	3. Rest of body

Answers: 1. lip, mouth; 2. thigh, knee; 3. chest, back

ETpedia: Materials Writing © Pavilion Publishing and Media Ltd and its licensors 2017.

Unit 7

8. Pairs of words

When dealing with words that might be confused or which are part of a wider lexical set, you can write exercises where the students have to try to explain the difference to each other. This is a useful speaking activity as well as one that targets the vocabulary. This example is from a lesson on the topic of families.

Work in pairs. Explain the difference between ...

- *a stepfather and a father-in-law*
- *a nephew and a cousin*
- *a grandmother and a great-grandmother*

---

9. Ranking

After providing controlled practice exercises with correct or incorrect answers, an exercise which asks the students to rank words according to their own opinion provides an interesting alternative. Ranking exercises also generate discussion because the students can try to agree on the order in pairs or groups. Here is an example exercise from a lesson on the topic of watching TV.

Put these kinds of TV show in order from the most interesting to the most boring for you. Then compare with a partner.

| *reality show* | *talk show* | *crime and suspense* | *nature documentary* | *soap opera* | *evening news* |

---

10. Personal and real-life examples

When writing in-class materials which can have open-ended answers for the teacher to check, it's always useful to end with an exercise that gets the students to personalise the new vocabulary. This example comes from material teaching the vocabulary for describing places where people live.

Write an example of each of the following.

- a *capital city* that you would like to visit
- a *village* close to where you live
- the name of one of the *suburbs* of a city you know

Unit 7

10 types of pronunciation exercise

When writing exercises to help students with different aspects of pronunciation, you will probably need to record certain sets of words or sentences. Typically, the students listen to the recording and then complete an exercise on the page or on screen. Here are 10 exercise types you could write which would be accompanied by a recording. They might be used in class, but would also work well in self-study materials. (Note that the audio script for each exercise type is given in brackets afterwards. With some types of exercise this also acts as the answer key and provides notes on how to say the word or sentence with certain stress patterns.) In most cases, the exercise type would work with or could be adapted for any aspect of pronunciation. Note that these examples are extracts, not the complete exercise; in most cases, you would probably have around eight words or eight sentences per exercise.

1. Repetition

Listen and repeat.
do, down, door, dear, done
Audio: do, down, door, dear, done

2. Identify a word

Listen and underline the word you hear.				
1. do/too	2. down/town	3. door/tore	4. dear/tear	5. done/ton
Audio: 1. do 2. town 3. door 4. dear 5. ton				

3. Identify a word in a sentence

Listen and underline the word you hear in the sentences.
1. I send/sent you an email.
2. She's riding/writing to you now.
3. We're waiting/wading in the river.
Audio: 1. I sent you an email. 2. She's writing to you now. 3. We're wading in the river.

Unit 8

4. Identifying sounds

Listen to these sentences. Does the speaker pronounce the /d/ sound at the end of the word with 'd'?

1. I love rock and roll music.   Yes/No

2. We cleaned the whole room.   Yes/No

3. Fish and chips are famous in the UK.   Yes/No

4. Did you see Sally?   Yes/No

Audio: 1. I love rock an(d) roll. 2. We cleaned the whole room. 3. Fish an(d) chips are famous in the UK. 4. Did you see Sally?

5. Categorising

Listen and put these verbs ending in 'd' in the table.

played walked sorted waited danced lived		
/d/	/t/	/ɪd/

Audio: played, walked, sorted, waited, danced, lived

Answers: /d/ played, lived, /t/ walked, danced, /ɪd/ sorted, waited

6. Stressed syllables

Listen to the words and underline the stressed syllable. Then listen again and repeat.

ambitious   determined   motivated   reliable   confident

Audio: am<u>bi</u>tious de<u>ter</u>mined <u>mo</u>tivated re<u>li</u>able <u>con</u>fident

7. Mark the intonation

Listen to the intonation at the end of the sentence. Does the speaker sound certain or uncertain? Mark the intonation up [➚] or down [➘]

1. You know Peter, don't you?

2. He's away on business today, isn't he?

3. I can call you at work, can't I?

Audio:
1. You know Peter, don't you? ➘

2. He's away on business today, isn't he? ➚

3. I can call you at work, can't I? ➘

8. Linking in sentences

Listen to sentences with linking. Write in the links.

1. Pick up Oliver's bag, please.

2. Did you send Ann an email?

3. Get out of this room immediately!

Audio:
1. Pick_up_Oliver's bag, please.
2. Did she send_Ann_an_email?
3. Get_out_of this room_immediately!

9. Contracted words

Listen to these sentences and circle any contracted words (had → 'd).

1. If I had had more time, I would have finished the exam.

2. I will only come in when they have left.

3. Their plane is landing at 12 and then they are taking a taxi.

Audio:
1. If I'd had more time, I would've finished the exam.
2. I'll only come in when they've left.
3. Their plane's landing at 12 and then they're taking a taxi.

Unit 8

10. Stressed words

Listen and underline the word with the most stress in each sentence.

1. That looks delicious!

2. What an amazing story!

3. We had a fantastic weekend!

Audio:

1. That looks <u>delicious</u>!

2. What an <u>amazing</u> story!

3. We had a <u>fantastic</u> weekend!

"A well-written piece of pronunciation material makes something complex seem simple. I like this metaphor: 'The better the diver, the smaller the splash'."

Mark Hancock, pronunciation book author, hancockmcdonald.com

10 tips for writing a controlled practice exercise

When you write a controlled practice exercise, such as a gap-fill or multiple-choice activity, you need to consider how the exercise will work as a whole, and the relationship between each of the questions within it. Here is an example of a controlled practice exercise, followed by 10 tips which outline the basic principles a materials writer should follow.

Past simple and present perfect

Write the verbs in brackets in the past simple or present perfect tense.

1. I _have lived_ (live) in my house for 10 years.
2. She _____ (work) here for three years, but now she works for another company.
3. My father _____ (go) to Spain for three weeks. He's back next week.
4. We _____ (not/see) you at the party. Were you there?
5. They _____ (not/left) yet. They're still here.
6. _____ you_____ (be) to Hong Kong?
7. When _____ you_____ (leave) school?
8. Where _____ they_____ (stay) on holiday? Was it nice?

Answer key: 2. *worked*; 3. *has gone*; 4. *didn't see*; 5. *haven't left*; 6. *Have, been*; 7. *did, leave*; 8. *did, stay*

---

1. Headings

It is important to make the aim of the exercise clear, so adding a heading can help. If the aim is to practise a grammar point, perhaps use that as the heading (eg Countable and uncountable nouns). For a vocabulary focus it might be the lexical set (eg Clothes) or the area of vocabulary (eg Verb + noun collocations).

2. Rubrics

Rubrics are the instructions we put at the beginning of an exercise. Teachers and students read them, so they need to be short and clear. Avoid more than one instruction per sentence. (See also Units 29 and 30.)

3. Give an example

Materials writers often include the first answer in this kind of exercise. It gives the students an example of what is required, so if they haven't understood the rubric, they will still probably know what to do because question 1. has been done for them.

4. Numbers and letters for referencing

Each question, sentence or gap in the exercise needs a number (eg 1 to 8). This helps classroom management for the teacher in a class and it also helps the teacher or students when checking the answers using an answer key. Note that it may not be necessary for online self-study materials or when writing directly into a template.

ETpedia: Materials Writing © Pavilion Publishing and Media Ltd and its licensors 2017.

Unit 9

5. Choice of answers

Where your gap-fill offers choice, make this clear. In the example above, the choice is between two tenses only. With other types of exercises, there might be more than two choices. Note that the more choices you offer, the more likely it is that the task becomes more difficult or has more than one answer.

6. Only test the target language

In the example exercise above, the target language is just the two tenses. It's important, therefore, not to use any vocabulary in the questions which the students are unlikely to know, because that would change the focus of the exercise.

7. Contexts and world knowledge

Following on from 6 and the idea that the sentences shouldn't include any new words that will interrupt the students' focus on the target language, the context of the sentences shouldn't be too obscure or include references to unknown content. This is so that the students are being tested on their grammar, not their general knowledge. For example, notice in the sample exercise above that the sentences refer to everyday information that most students will know or be familiar with.

8. Eight

Typically, eight is a good number of gaps for one exercise. This isn't a fixed rule, but it's a good guideline. Six gaps will often seem too few and unchallenging, especially if one is already done as an example, whilst exercises with 10 gaps or more can sometimes become monotonous for the students.

9. Affirmative, negative, questions

You need variety in the exercise and – especially with verb-based grammar exercises – it's a good idea to include a range of sentences in the affirmative and negative as well as question forms.

10. Answer key

If you are producing the exercise for your own use, you probably don't need an answer key. However, the advantage of writing an answer key is that it's a quick way to test that the exercise works and that you haven't made any mistakes. Better still, ask a colleague to try the exercise before you use it in class. If you are also writing the exercise to be used by others, they might appreciate an answer key as well. Note also that if you are writing the exercise for computer-based materials, the program will automatically require you enter the correct answer.

10 types of gap-fill questions in sentences

When you write a series of gap-fill exercises for students, especially in self-study materials, you will want to vary the style of the activity. Here are 10 different examples of types of gap-fill sentences to help you achieve variety in your writing. Each example is taken from a different exercise, with the original rubric given in bold.

1. Basic gap-fill

Here you take out a word, which the students have to write in.

Write in the missing word.

I live _____ England.

2. A choice of words

Here, the gaps have to all be filled by two or three different words.
Give the options, and the students complete the gaps.

Write in the correct preposition: at, on, in.

They're arriving _____ three o'clock.

3. With the first letter

Here you take out a word, but you provide the first letter at the beginning of the gap to help students guess the word.

Write in the missing word.

W_____ you like a cup of tea?

4. Using the word in brackets

Here you gap a word, but you provide the missing word in brackets next to the gap. The students have to change the form of the word (usually a verb) to complete the gap.

Write the word in brackets in the past simple or present perfect tense.

I _____ (work) for that company in 2001.

I _____ (live) here since 2001.

5. Double gap

Here you provide two different sentences with the same word missing in each. Students have to complete the two gaps with the same word.

The same word is missing in both sentences. Write it in.

I always _____ my lunch break at midday.

I usually _____ a shower before I go to bed.

---

6. Listen and complete.

Here you take out a word, which students have to complete after hearing it in context.

Listen to the conversation and write in the missing words.

A: Are you going to the _____ tonight?

B: Yes, with a friend. We're going to see the new Star Wars _____.

---

7. Definitions

Here the gap is the key word in the definition of the word.

Match the jobs to the definitions.

teacher   nurse   dentist

A _____ helps students to learn in school.

A _____ checks your teeth.

A _____ looks after people in hospital.

---

8. Two gaps per sentence

Here you remove two words from a series of sentences. Provide the pairs of words to the students, who have to put them back into the right gaps.

Complete each sentence with a pair of words.

Can + salt   Could + hand   Would + join

_____ you like to _____ us for dinner?

_____ you pass the _____?

_____ you give me a _____?

Unit 10

9. Personalised gaps (without one correct answer)

Here the missing word is more open, to allow for personalised answers.

Write in your own words.

My favourite food is _____.

My favourite drink is_____.

My favourite sport is_____.

10. Students write their own gaps

Here you turn the exercise on its head, and ask students to make the sentences and gap the words.

Write five sentences with gaps to test your partner. Miss out these words in your gaps: *TV, desk, wallet, pen, book.*

Answers for questions in 1–8: 1. in, 2. at, 3. Would, 4. worked/'ve lived, 5. have, 6. cinema/film, 7. teacher/dentist/nurse, 8. Would + join/Can + salt/Could + hand

Unit 10

In Unit 10, the examples of gap-fills were in isolated sentences. We also use gap-fills in longer texts. To illustrate the different ways to do this, here is the first paragraph of a longer text about the history of parliament and democracy. The 10 examples of gap-fills in texts are all based on parts of this text.

> *It is said that democracy began in Ancient Greece where people first had the right to vote on how they were governed. In fact, only certain men were allowed to vote but, after the Greeks, other civilisations also developed their own forms of democracy. For example, the Vikings set up the Icelandic Parliament called the Althing in 930 AD. It claims to be the first parliament in the world and continues to the present day.*

1. Gap words at regular intervals

You can put gaps into the text at regular intervals; for example, every eighth word can be missing.

Write in the missing words.

It is said that democracy began in (1)_____ Greece where people first had the right (2)_____ vote on how they were governed. In (3)_____, only certain men were allowed to vote (4)_____, after the Greeks, other civilisations also developed (5)_____ own forms of democracy.

Answers: 1. Ancient, 2. to, 3. fact, 4. but, 5. their

2. Target a grammar item

As an alternative to the example in 1, you can choose certain words which are connected in some way, or words which you have been teaching recently.

Write in the correct form of the verb *to be*.

It (1)___ said that democracy began in Ancient Greece where people first had the right to vote on how they (2)_____ governed. In fact, only certain men (3)_____ allowed to vote but, after the Greeks, other civilisations also developed their own forms of democracy. For example, the Vikings set up the Icelandic Parliament called the Althing in 930 AD. It claims (4)_____ the first parliament in the world and continues to the present day.

Answers: (1) is, (2) were, (3) were, (4) to be

3. Words in brackets

This type of exercise is especially useful when you want the students to practise making tense changes or changes to the form of a word (eg adjective to noun).

Write the verbs in brackets in the passive form.

It is (1)_____ (say) that democracy began in Ancient Greece where people first had the right to vote on how they were (2)_____ (govern). In fact, only certain men were (3)_____ (allow) to vote but, after the Greeks, other civilisations also developed their own forms of democracy.

Answers: (1) said, (2) governed, (3) allowed

Unit 11

4. Multiple-choice

Choose the missing word from A, B and C.

It is said that democracy began in Ancient Greece where people first had the right to (1)___ on how they were governed. In fact, only certain men were allowed to vote but, after the Greeks, other civilisations also developed their own forms of democracy. For example, the Vikings (2)____ up the Icelandic Parliament called the Althing in 930 AD. It claims to be the first parliament in the world and continues to the (3)___ day.

(1) A vote B law C elect
(2) A grew B set C made
(3) A new B next C present

Answers: (1) A, (2) B, (3) C

5. Choose from a lexical set

The following type of exercise is useful for introducing and practising sets of words related to a particular topic.

Use the words in the box to complete the gaps.

democracy	right	parliament	civilisations	vote

It is said that (1)_____ began in Ancient Greece where people first had the (2)_____ to vote on how they were governed. In fact, only certain men were allowed to (3)_____ but, after the Greeks, other (4)_____ also developed their own form of democracy. For example, the Vikings set up the Icelandic Parliament called the Althing in 930 AD. It claims to be the first (5)_____ in the world and continues to the present day.

Answers: (1) democracy, (2) right, (3) vote, (4) civilisations, (5) parliament

6. Gaps with a clue

This is a useful variation and works well for focusing on words such as auxiliary verbs, determiners and prepositions.

The missing words all have two letters. Write them in.

It (1)____ said that democracy began (2)____ Ancient Greece where people first had the right (3)_____ vote on how they were governed.

Answers: (1) is, (2) in, (3) to

7. Word form gaps

This exercise appears in certain types of examination (eg the Cambridge First) and is useful for looking at different word forms in context.

Write the word at the end in the correct form.
It is said that (1)_____ began in Ancient Greece where people first had the right to   DEMOCRAT *vote on how they were (2)_____. In fact, only certain men were allowed to vote*   GOVERN *but, after the Greeks, other (3)_____ also developed their own form of democracy.*   CIVILISED
Answers: (1) democracy, (2) governed, (3) Civilisations

8. Gapped letters

This exercise focuses students on spelling and accuracy.

Write in the missing vowels.
*It is said that (1) **d_m_cr_cy** began in Ancient Greece where people first had the right to vote on how they were (2) **g_v_rn_d**. In fact, only certain men were allowed to vote but, after the Greeks, other (3) **c_v_l_s_t_ _ns** also developed their own form of democracy.*
Answers: (1) democracy, (2) governed, (3) civilisations

9. Find the gap

Both this type of exercise and the next (10) have no marked gap. As a result, the students have to work harder at checking the text for the missing word or for accuracy.

Write the word at the end in the correct position in the sentence.
It is said that democracy in Ancient Greece where people first had the right to on   BEGAN *how they were governed. In fact, only certain men were allowed to vote but, after*   VOTE *the Greeks, civilisations also developed their form of democracy. For example, the*   OTHER *Vikings set up the Icelandic Parliament called the Althing in 930 AD.*   OWN
Answers: democracy **began** in, to **vote** on, Greeks, **other** civilisations, their **own** form

10. Delete the extra word

Each line in the paragraph contains one extra and incorrect word. Delete it.
It is said by that democracy began in Ancient Greece where people first had the right to vote on how they were governed. In fact, only certain men were allowed to be vote but, after the Greeks, other civilisations also developed their own themselves form of democracy. For example, the Vikings set up the Icelandic Parliament called the Althing in 930 AD. It is claims to be the first the parliament in the world and continues to the present day.
Answers: Line 1: <u>by</u> that, Line 2: <u>be</u> vote, Line 3: <u>own</u> themselves, Line 4: It <u>is</u>, Line 5: <u>the</u> parliament

10 types of multiple-choice questions

Like gap-fill questions, multiple-choice questions are for controlled practice, and you'll probably use them when you write tests. Sometimes we think that multiple-choice questions are a bit of a dull exercise type to use in materials, but they are helpful for checking that the students understand the target language. From the selection below, you can also see that the materials writer has a wide choice of multiple-choice question types. (Some of these are similar to the gap-fill exercises in Unit 10.) There is more on how multiple-choice questions can be used in reading and listening comprehension question writing in Units 19 and 22.

1. Choose from A, B and C

In this type of question, there is a gap in the sentence and three choices are provided below.

Choose from A, B and C.
I____ from Brazil.
A am   B is   C are

2. Choose the correct word in italics

Here there is no gap, but the three choices are provided *in situ* in the sentence, usually in italics to distinguish the choices from the surrounding sentence.

Choose the correct word in italics.
They *am/is/are* Brazilian.

3. Match the correct ending

This is very similar to type A, except the end of the sentence is gapped and there may be more than one word in the answer. This kind of question is good for word order or verb forms.

Match the correct ending.
Why don't you ____
A try the soup?
B to try the soup?
C trying the soup?

ETpedia: Materials Writing © Pavilion Publishing and Media Ltd and its licensors 2017.

4. Match the two halves of the sentences

This is almost more of a matching activity than a traditional multiple choice. Three options are provided but each corresponds to one other option.

Match the two halves of the sentences.

1. Why don't	a) trying the soup?
2. How about	b) try the soup.
3. Let's	c) you try the soup?

5. Choose the objects you normally find in each place

In this kind of question, a context is provided (in this case, place) and students need to choose from a group of words which ones could be found in that context.

Choose the objects you normally find in each place.

1. School

a) pens	b) board	c) bath	d) wardrobe

2. Bank

a) television	b) money	c) cash machine	d) blanket

3. Bedroom

a) sheets	b) printer	c) carpet	d) calculator

6. Complete the sentences with a, an, the or no article (–)

Here the choice of answers are the same for each gap.

Complete the sentences with a, an, the or no article (–).

1. Sara lives in _____ United States.

2. Joel works in _____ office.

3. Raul goes to work by _____ bike.

4. Taylor doesn't have _____ job.

Unit 12

7. Tick the correct sentence

In this kind of question, the choice is not for words within a sentence but for the sentences themselves.

Tick the correct sentence.

A. I live here since 2002.

B. I lived here since 2002.

C. I've lived here since 2002.

---

8. Tick the correct picture

This kind of multiple-choice question works best for vocabulary, and takes up more space. Instead of choosing from word options, the student must choose from picture options.

Tick the correct picture.

'She missed the bus.'

A  B  C

---

9. Tick the polite and correct response

In this kind of activity the choice is more about register as well as grammatical correctness.

Tick the polite and correct response.

'It was nice of you to help me move those boxes.'

A. 'Of course.'

B. 'No problem. You're welcome.'

C. 'Yes, it was, wasn't it?'

---

10. Odd one out

Here a choice of words (or phrases) is provided and students need to eliminate the one that doesn't belong.

Look at these groups of words. Delete the incorrect word in the group and say why.

1. bathroom, kitchen, ~~café~~, toilet, living room (*the other words are in someone's house*)

2. tram, bus, train, aeroplane, taxi, station

3. plate, salt, knife, fork, bowl

Answers for questions in 1–10: 1. A, 2. are, 3. A, 4. 1c, 2a, 3b, 5. 1a and b, 2b and c, 3a and c, 6. 1. the, 2. an, 3. - ,4. a, 7. C, 8. A, 9. B, 10. 2. station – the other words are all types of transportation, 3. salt – the other words are utensils you use to eat with

---

"We tend to take writing multiple-choice questions for granted, but it is surprisingly easy to get them wrong. Watch out for common problems such as making one answer much longer than the others or having two answers which are both correct."

Evan Frendo, ELT materials writer

10 types of re-ordering exercises

There are various types of language exercises which are based around the idea of reordering something correctly. As these 10 examples demonstrate, reordering can be anything from putting individual letters in order to make a single word through to ordering complete sentences in a conversation.

1. Reordering spelling

Reorder the letters to make animal words.

1. olin _____

2. phanelet _____

3. larigol _____

Answers: lion, elephant, gorilla

2. Reordering by size

Put the animal words in order from the smallest animal to the largest.

| lion | ant | elephant | tortoise | mouse |

Answers: ant, mouse, tortoise, lion, elephant

3. Reordering by sequence

Put these sequences in the correct order.

1. Tuesday, Friday, Saturday, Monday, Thursday, Sunday, Wednesday

2. March, February, December, January, June, August, July, April, October, May, September, November

3. twenties, early fifties, teens, late forties, late sixties, mid-thirties

Answers:
1. Sunday, Monday, Tuesday, Wednesday, Thursday, Friday, Saturday
2. January, February, March, April, May, June, July, August, September, October, November, December
3. teens, twenties, mid-thirties, late forties, early fifties, late sixties

ETpedia: Materials Writing © Pavilion Publishing and Media Ltd and its licensors 2017.

4. Reordering by strength

Put these words in order from the hottest to the coldest:
boiling   freezing   chilly   hot   warm
Answer: boiling, hot, warm, chilly, freezing

5. Reordering by percentages

Write these adverbs in the correct place on the scale: *hardly ever*, *always*, *sometimes*, *never*, *often*.
100%<--->0%   1   2   3   4   5
Answer: 1. always, 2. often, 3. sometimes, 4. hardly ever, 5. never

6. Putting actions in a logical order

Put these activities in the order you do them. Then compare with a partner.
leave school   have dinner   go to bed   get up   have breakfast   do homework
take a bath or shower   go to school   have lunch   watch TV or a film

7. Reordering sentences

Put the words in the correct order to make expressions.
1. you do think what?
2. can I a you for second interrupt?
3. I what you see mean.
4. up to agree with I you a point.
Answers: 1. What do you think? 2. Can I interrupt you for a second? 3. I see what you mean. 4. I agree with you up to a point.

Unit 13

8. Reordering sentences with a target word.

Put the words in the correct order to make sentences with *too*.

1. like / **too** / pizza / I

2. eat / much / don't / **too**

3. homework / **too** / my / is / difficult

Answers: 1. I like pizza, too. 2. Don't eat too much. 3. My homework is too difficult.

9. Reordering conversations

Put the lines of this telephone dialogue in the correct order.

_____a Hi, Michael. It's Vanessa.

_____b I know. I've been really busy.

_____c Hello. Michael speaking.

_____d Vanessa! How are you? We haven't spoken in ages.

Answers: 1.c, 2.a, 3.d, 4.b

10. Reordering texts by paragraph

You can cut up longer texts or edit them so that the paragraphs are in the wrong order. The students have to read the text and number the paragraphs correctly. See also Unit 19.

ETpedia: Materials Writing © Pavilion Publishing and Media Ltd and its licensors 2017.

Unit 13

10 types of categorisation exercise

Writing exercises that ask the students to put words, phrases and expressions into groups or categories can be a useful way of encouraging them to think about language. These exercises can focus on the grammatical forms of words, on the way they are used or on the meaning. You can also use a categorisation exercise to focus on pronunciation. Below are 10 example exercises. You can adapt these to suit your own context. The first few exercise types illustrate how we use categorisation with different areas of language. Some of the activities involve labelling words or phrases; others involve putting them into a table. The last two exercise types have a freer element and add some variety. In 9, the students decide how to group the words, and although there is probably an expected answer, it's possible that they might come up with other categories. The final exercise adds a competitive element in which the students see how many words they can think of to fit a given category.

1. Functional phrases

> **Which of these things does a waiter say in a restaurant? Which does the customer say? Write *W* or *C*.**
>
> 1. Would you like to see the menu?
>
> 2. Are there any specials this evening?
>
> 3. Are you ready to order?
>
> 4. Can I have the bill, please?
>
> 5. I'll have the fish.
>
> 6. Have you seen the specials?
>
> Answers: 1. W, 2. C, 3. W, 4. C, 5. C, 6. W

2. Register

> **Decide if these phrases are formal, informal or neutral. Write *F*, *I* or *N*.**
>
> 1 What's up?
>
> 2 How are you?
>
> 3 It's a pleasure to meet you.
>
> 4 Nice to meet you.
>
> 5 I'd be delighted to join you.
>
> 6 How are you doing?
>
> Answers: 1. I, 2. N, 3. F, 4. N, 5. F, 6. I

3. Vocabulary

Put the words into two groups: things you wear on your feet (write *F*) and things you wear on your head (write *H*).

socks	helmet	slippers	cap	turban	sandals	flip flops	hood

Answers: Feet: socks, slippers, sandals, flip flops; Head: helmet, cap, turban, hood

4. Meaning

Put this language for describing trends into the correct columns of the table.

increase	decrease	remain steady	go up	fall	rise	drop	stay the same

↑	↓	→

Answers: ↑: increase, go up, rise; ↓: decrease, fall, drop →: remain steady, stay the same

5. Collocation

Put these words under the correct verb in the table.

swimming	yoga	football	hockey	skiing	karate

PLAY	DO	GO

Answers: play football/hockey; do yoga/karate; go swimming/skiing

6. Grammar

Put the verbs into two groups: regular verbs (write *R*) and irregular verbs (write *I*).

give	kick	stand	dance	drop	go	want	buy

Answers: Regular: kick, dance, drop, want; Irregular: give, stand, go, buy

7. Pronunciation

Categorise these words by word stress.

Germany	Argentina	Switzerland	Poland	Kuwait	Japan	England

● ●	● ● ●	● ●	● ● ● ●

Answers: ● ●: Poland/England, ● ● ●: Germany, ● ●: Kuwait/Japan, ● ● ● ●: Argentina

8. Venn diagrams

Put the types of clothing into the correct part of the diagram.

blouse	dinner jacket	dress	hat	shirt
skirt	sock	three-piece suit		tie

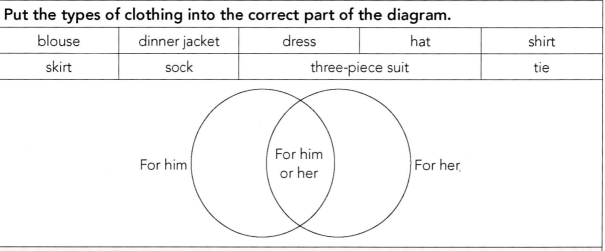

For him

For him or her

For her

Answers: For him: dinner jacket, tie, three-piece suit; For him or her: shirt, hat, sock; For her: blouse, skirt, dress

9. Students decide

Put the words into three groups. You decide the groups. Be prepared to explain your answers.

carrot   mushroom   bean   tomato   coffee   onion   orange   milk   juice

Possible answer: vegetables, fruit, drinks

10. Competitive

Write as many words as you can for each category in one minute. Then compare with a partner.

Things you find in the kitchen

Things you find in the bedroom

Things you find in the living room

Unit 14

10 sentence transformation questions

Sentence transformations involve rewriting sentences using different words but maintaining the same meaning. Students often find them difficult to do – and writers often find them challenging to write.

In the most basic form of sentence transformation, you provide a complete sentence and part of a second sentence. The students have to complete the second sentence so that it has the same meaning as the first, but using different words or a different grammatical form. For example, with the passive form you could write a question like this.

Charles Hull invented the first 3D printer in 1984.

The first 3D printer_____Charles Hull in 1984.

Answer: *The first 3D printer was invented by Charles Hull in 1984.*

However, in sentence transformations written for higher-level material and exams, the question often includes a word in bold which the students must include in their sentence, and there is often a word limit. Sentence transformations with a given word tend to lend themselves to testing certain language items. The 10 examples below are categorised according to the language items most commonly practised with this question type. A typical rubric might be: **Complete the second sentence so that it has a similar meaning to the first sentence. Use between two and five words, including the word given without changing it**.

1. The passive form

Which building did the architect Norman Foster design?

BY

Which building _____Norman Foster?

2. Alternatives to *if*

They'll only know if we tell them.

UNLESS

They _____them.

3. Past modals

It wasn't a good idea to set off without a torch.

SHOULD

We _____without a torch.

4. Cause and effect

As a result of the flooding, all the residents had to be evacuated.

BECAUSE

The residents had to be evacuated _____ flooding.

5. Comparative forms

Her exam results were lower than her teacher expected.

AS

Her exam results _____ her teacher expected.

6. Reported speech

'Please complete this report before midday,' his boss said.

TOLD

His boss _____ the report before midday.

7. Phrasal verbs

The builders discovered the ancient walls when they started building an office block.

CAME

The builders _____ when they started building an office block.

8. Synonyms

Can you take care of my cat while I'm away?

LOOK

Can you _____ cat while I'm away?

9. Functional expressions

How about inviting everyone over next week?

DON'T

Why _____ everyone over next week?

10. Lexical items

Can you turn the TV off?

MIND

Would _____ the TV off?

Answers:
1. Which building was designed by Norman Foster?
2. They won't know unless we tell them.
3. We shouldn't have set off without a torch.
4. The residents had to be evacuated because of (the) flooding.
5. Her exam results weren't as high as her teacher expected.
6. His boss told him to complete the report before midday.
7. The builders came across the ancient walls when they started building an office block.
8. Can you look after my cat while I'm away?
9. Why don't you/we invite everyone over next week?
10. Would you mind turning the TV off?

Unit 15

10 types of error correction exercises

Exercises which ask the students to identify and correct language errors are very useful because they draw the students' attention to common mistakes. However, some teachers dislike this exercise type because they think that the students assume that anything on the written page will always be accurate, and they believe that seeing errors in texts may lead the students into making mistakes that they wouldn't otherwise have made. To ensure there is no confusion, you need to make sure that your exercise instructions (ie rubrics) are clear and that the first error is always clearly indicated, as an example of what the students are required to do.

Here are 10 examples of exercise types you can write which ask the students to identify an error. The first six are exercises that focus on errors in single words and sentences. The remaining four are exercise types you might write for higher-level students; they involve error correction in paragraphs and longer texts.

1. Spot the spelling mistakes

To produce a basic error correction exercise, you can list some commonly misspelt words for your students to correct. Alternatively, embed them in a text. Here is an example:

Each word has a mistake. Write the words correctly.

1. ~~acommodation~~ accommodation

2. greatful _____

3. recieve _____

4. untill _____

Answers: 2. grateful, 3. receive, 4. until

---

2. Add the punctuation

Most exercises practising punctuation will involve an element of error correction. You could write a text with no punctuation and ask the students to rewrite it correctly like this:

Write this text correctly. Add capital letters, full stops, commas and apostrophes.

Jake

~~jake~~ and sam lived in an apartment in madrid where theyd been for five weeks every day they got up at eight, had breakfast in the café round the corner and went to their spanish lessons

Answer: *Jake and Sam lived in an apartment in Madrid, where they'd been for five weeks. Every day they got up at eight, had breakfast in the café round the corner and went to their Spanish lessons.*

---

3. Correct the sentence

You can write sentences containing one word that demonstrates a typical mistake. You could base your exercise on the types of mistakes your students frequently make.

Correct ONE word in each sentence.

     and
1. I love pizza ~~but~~ I like pasta.

2. I would of come if I'd had time.

3. She said me she was leaving.

4. I'm agree with you.

Answers: 2. I would have come if I'd had time. 3. She said she was leaving (or She told me she was leaving). 4. I agree with you.

---

4. Is it right or wrong?

As a variation to the exercise in 3, you can also include some sentences which are correct, so the students first have to decide if the sentence is correct or not before making any necessary correction. This is a way of adding an element of difficulty, and it is useful when designing materials for different levels. So the exercise in 3 might look like this.

Which sentences are correct? Tick (✔) the correct sentences and put a cross (✗) next to the incorrect sentences. Then correct the incorrect sentences.

     and
1. I love pizza ~~but~~ I like pasta. (✗)

2. I would have come if I'd had time.

3. She said she was leaving.

4. I'm agree with you.

Answers: 2. ✔   3. ✔   4. ✗ I agree with you.

---

5. Tick the correct sentence

One form of error correction exercise is multiple-choice. The students have to choose between the same sentence written in different ways. They tick the one that is correct. For example:

Compare the two sentences in each pair. Tick the correct sentence.	
1. a I would of come if I'd had time.	b I would have come if I'd had time.
2. a I'm sorry but he's out.	b I'm afraid but he's out.
3. a It's been here for years.	b It's been here since years.
Answers: 1.b, 2.a, 3.a	

6. Spot the extra incorrect word

You can write a text and add an extra incorrect word to each line. This type of question appears in certain types of examinations.

Write the extra incorrect word at the end of each line.	
In a recent survey of internet users, researchers found that most ~~the~~ people	*the*
spend between three to four hours a day going to online. The majority of the	_____
respondents used their mobile phones though the results are depended on age.	_____
Answers:	
spend between three to four hours a day going ~~to~~ online. The majority of the	*to*
respondents used their mobile phones, though the results ~~are~~ depended on age.	*are*

7. Spot correct lines and incorrect words

When writing higher-level materials, you can add to the level of difficulty in the example in 6 by not having a mistake in every line. Your rubric might read: **Some lines in this paragraph are correct and some lines have an extra incorrect word. Tick the correct lines and write the extra word after each incorrect line.**

Unit 16

8. Spot the mistakes

To increase the level of difficulty even further when using a text for error correction exercises, just provide the text and add in a certain number of mistakes. These can appear anywhere, including within the same line as another mistake. This provides a useful proof-reading task for higher-level students. Here is the text in 6, adapted for higher-levels:

There are three extra words in this text that you don't need. Find and delete them.

In a recent survey of internet users, researchers found that most the people spend between three to four hours a day going to online. The majority of the respondents used their mobile phones, though the results are depended on age.

---

9. Identify the type of error

Another challenge for higher-level students is to identify the type of mistake in a text. So instead of just spotting it and correcting it, they also have to say what kind of error it is. Sometimes course materials will include an error code which the students learn to recognise and use. Here are some common symbols: *Sp = spelling mistake, WO = incorrect word order, P = punctuation mistake, T = mistake with verb tenses.*

This type of exercise is especially useful for teachers if they intend to mark their students' writing using an error code. Here's an example of how you might write such an exercise:

Find the mistakes in this paragraph. Underline the error and write the type of error at the end of the line.

In a recent survey of <u>users internet</u>, researchers found that most people	1. *WO*
spend between three to four hours a day going online. the majority of the	2. _____
respondents used their mobile phones for web browsing.	3. _____

Answers: 2. P ('the' needs a capital letter), 3. Sp (respondents not respondants)

---

10. Self correction and peer correction

The previous nine types of error correction exercise all involve students identifying errors in an exercise. It's also useful to include error correction exercises that make them look at their own writing for errors. So when students complete a writing task, you can add a rubric such as: *Now check your writing for any errors.* If the previous exercises in the materials for the lesson had a particular language focus, then the rubric can be more targeted like this: Now check your writing for correct use of the past simple. You can also write a rubric to encourage peer correction, like this: *Work in pairs. Swap your writing and read your partner's work. Give feedback and circle any errors. Discuss these with your partner.*

Unit 16

Writing materials for reading, listening, speaking and writing

The previous section of this book presented basic exercises involving language practice at sentence level or in short paragraphs. In this section, we will move on to look at how you can create more extensive materials to develop your students' four skills. These demand a wider range of materials writing skills.

The first few units on the receptive skills (reading and listening) provide help with identifying and selecting different texts. When necessary, writers will need to create whole texts from scratch or adapt them from existing texts. These texts will be used to check the students' comprehension, so once a text is written or chosen, the materials writer needs to devise a set of comprehension questions based on that text.

The second part of this section looks at writing for the productive skills (speaking and writing). Creating exercises to practise speaking can be especially challenging, and you'll find a number of tips to help you, with a special focus on writing role plays. The final units on writing skills list some typical question types commonly found in course materials and also in examinations. There are also ideas for writing exercises which help students develop their subskills.

10 criteria for selecting a reading text

When looking for reading texts that are suitable for use as language teaching material, there are various issues to consider. In the 10 criteria below, the obvious points are that a text needs to include language that is relevant and at the right kind of level. At the same time, a text needs to be engaging, with an interest level that will appeal to a wide number of students.

1. Topic

When looking for a text to use in your reading classes, your obvious starting point is the topic area you are currently working on. So if the lesson is on sport, you'll probably start looking in the sports pages of a newspaper or on sports-related websites. If you're looking for an academic topic, you'll want to find a reliable and accurate source to ensure the quality of the information.

2. Target language

Once you have found a text related to your chosen topic, you need to make sure that it includes your target language. So, for example, if you find a text about sport, it is likely to include a range of sports-related vocabulary, but there is no guarantee that it will include the target language you need it to present. Sometimes you may select a text because it features the key language you need – and the topic is slightly secondary. Always be on the lookout for texts that typically feature certain key language. For example, you will often find the present simple tense in texts which are about a day in the life of a famous person; *will* for future prediction often appears in articles about science and technology.

3. The interest factor

As mentioned above, a good materials writer looks for texts that relate to the topic and to the target language. But the real challenge is to find a text which is also likely to be of interest to all the students in the class. Of course, you won't please all the people all the time – particularly when it comes to texts such as news articles, stories or anything that people choose to read, depending on their own personal tastes. What some students will find of interest, others will not, especially when a text is related to a particular topic.

One approach is to find texts that provide a fresh or original angle on a topic. This requires the writer to think more broadly around the topic. For example, for the topic of sport, instead of a text which is just about football or just about basketball, you might look for something more contentious, such as whether competitive sport in school is a good or bad thing. The ability to use search engines effectively will really aid this kind of research.

4. A model

So far in this list of criteria, we have mainly referred to the selection of texts that appear in mainstream media. However, as well as using reading texts from newspapers, magazines or websites, you might be writing materials for students who need to work with reading texts that are similar to those they themselves may need to read or write in English for their academic or professional lives. So if the material is for use by business English students, it might be helpful to find examples of real emails which they can study before being asked to write their own emails.

5. Length of text

The number of words in a text may affect your choice, especially if it needs to reflect the length of text the students may have to deal with in an exam. If the text is longer, you will need to consider whether you can use only part of it or whether you could adapt it to make it shorter. On the other hand, if the text is too short, you may need to consider if there are ways to add words without losing the sense of the original text.

6. With images

Texts which are accompanied by images or visual elements are often used by materials writers because pictures make a text look less daunting to the students and can offer a way into the material. For example, a news article with an engaging photo allows the writer to include an activity in which the students discuss the photo and predict the contents of the text before reading. Technical or academic texts may have diagrams or graphs which also makes the text more accessible. (See also Unit 32 on images.)

7. Fact or opinion

Many texts, especially those taken from news sources and the web, tend either to be factual or to express views and opinions. Some contain a balance of both. Factual texts will suit lessons where you plan to set comprehension tasks in which the students scan the text for specific information. Texts with opinions lend themselves to higher-level reading tasks where the students need to infer the author's meaning.

8. Lifespan

One complaint about texts in coursebooks is that they can quickly go out of date. If they are about technology, that technology will look old after a couple of years. If they are about someone famous, there's always the danger that the person is well-known in some parts of the world or does something controversial. So if you plan on writing material that will need to be reused over months or even years, try to choose texts that won't date.

9. Culture

If you are choosing a text that will be used with students from different countries, consider whether it will work across cultures. For example, if the text refers to a movie that is famous in your own culture, don't assume it will be known elsewhere. Not everyone in the world watches films made in Hollywood or knows the names of celebrities who are familiar to you. That isn't to say you should avoid all texts with cultural references, but if there are cultural references, the text should explain the background so that the students will understand the relevance.

10. Controversy

One complaint that's often aimed at language teaching material is its lack of controversy. In other words, reading texts in coursebooks avoid anything that might offend some learners or provoke extreme opinions. There is even the term PARSNIP in ELT publishing; this is an acronym for a list of topics to be avoided: *politics*, *alcohol*, *religion*, *sex*, *narcotics*, *-isms* and *pork*. Topic avoidance only tends to affect materials which will be used in many different countries with different norms and values. However, even for materials aimed at learners in one country, sensitivity is needed with regard to what the students are expected to read and discuss. Not all students will feel comfortable expressing their personal, political or religious opinions and a text should not put teachers in the position of having to handle topics which they feel are too controversial.

(See also Unit 47 on 10 questions about copyright and permissions.)

"I like to choose texts where the teacher and the students learn something new about the world as well as learning English."

James Styring, teacher, trainer and author, UK

Unit 17

10 tips on adapting the level of a text

Although it is often suggested that using authentic reading texts with students at any level is better than using something adapted or specially written, the reality is that we often need to adjust the level of the language in authentic or high-level texts. In most cases, this means lowering the level of the language. Here are 10 tips on how to adapt a text. (Also see the example of text adaptation on page 69.)

1. Shorten the text

This is an obvious starting point when adapting the level of a text. In part, it will happen naturally as you simplify the language, but it's still worth doing a word count to ensure there has been a significant change to the length and, therefore, the level of challenge.

2. Simplify the sentence structure

With lower-level texts, writers generally use one clause per sentence. If there are two clauses, they only use simple conjunctions such as *and* or *but*. If you have a high-level text with lots of relative clauses, for example, you might need to edit them out.

3. Simplify the grammar structure

When adapting texts, you'll need to know what the students are expected to have learnt so far on the course. For example, if your text includes verbs in the passive form and your students have never seen this form before, you might rewrite the passive sentences to make them active.

4. Simplify text structure and cohesion

Not all authentic texts are written in a way that is well-structured. Sometimes it's necessary to make a text more cohesive by rearranging the way in which information is presented and adding in linking language such as *firstly, secondly, then, also, in addition*, etc.

5. Omitting low-frequency vocabulary

The higher the level of a reading text, the more likely it is to include low-frequency words. This might be useful for advanced students, but you will probably need to find a way to omit them for lower levels. If a word is crucial for understanding (in a text about something scientific, for example), it's often worth including a glossary with the text so that content-specific vocabulary can be quickly dealt with in class.

6. Using synonyms

Following on from 5, if you want to maintain the meaning behind certain vocabulary in a text, then you can reduce the level by replacing a higher-level word like *furious* or *boiling* with a lower-level synonym such as *angry* or *hot*.

7. Recycling language

When adapting and rewriting texts, always use the opportunity to recycle language that you know has been recently taught. So if your students have just covered a particular tense, try to incorporate some examples of that tense in your text.

8. Break the text into manageable parts

If you need to use a long, complex text (eg in materials designed to prepare the students for reading long academic texts), consider presenting it in stages. For example, you might

Unit 18

base a couple of comprehension exercises on only the first two paragraphs of the material. Then write new exercises based on the third and fourth paragraphs. By presenting the text in stages, you will make reading it seem more achievable.

9. Use glossaries

Sometimes you won't be able to omit difficult words which are crucial to understanding the whole text. This is particularly the case with technical or scientific material. If you don't need the students to use these words actively, only to recognise them, it is a good idea to add a glossary. For example, in a text on architecture which includes the term *steel girder*, you could simply define the term in a glossary, or even show a small picture of a girder.

10. Use online tools

There are a number of online tools that will analyse the contents of a text for you; some will even give you an idea of what percentage of the language is at a certain level. Most work on the basis that you copy and paste your text into the program, which then analyses it for you. Here are two well-known online tools which are popular with materials writers. (Type the names into a good search engine to find them.)

▶ The Oxford Textchecker (Oxford University Press)

This tool can check your text to see what percentage of the words are from the 2,000 or 3,000 most commonly-used words in the English language. It highlights any words not within these two lists. This is useful if you want to identify any vocabulary that needs to be omitted or changed.

▶ The English Vocabulary Profile (Cambridge University Press)

This tool can analyse the vocabulary in a text according to its CEFR level. It will tell you, for example, if a word in the text is normally taught and learnt at A1 level or A2 level. This allows you to adapt the text accordingly.

Note that such tools are not precise (though they are likely to become more so in the future) and need to be used carefully. Consider what they tell you alongside your own intuition as a teacher and what you know to be the case with the students who will use your materials.

"I often use textcheckers when I'm adapting an authentic text as a quick way of spotting words that might be above level and need changing or glossing. You have to be careful not to overlook the apparently 'easy', high-frequency words, though, and watch out for when they're used in a less obvious sense (eg the human body is marked as A1 on EVP, but an official body is C2) or when they're part of a tricky phrasal verb or idiom."

Julie Moore, ELT materials developer

Look at these three examples of the same text adapted for different levels. The first is a paragraph from an article about extreme weather. The second is the same text adapted for students at an intermediate level (B1/B2) and the third is for lower-level students (A2/B1).

Original text

There's been a change in the weather. Extreme events like Hurricane Katrina in 2005, which hit the coast of Louisiana in the USA, killing 1,830 people, are happening more frequently than they used to. Again in the US, in April 2011, around one hundred separate tornadoes hit six southern states, which led to loss of life and damage to property. Record heat waves have also been recorded across the globe. 2010 saw Moscow temperatures soar and forest wildfires burn out of control across Russia. Australia, too, has had its fair share of the heat, with summer temperatures reaching record highs and record droughts for the last decade.

Intermediate level text

There's been a change in the weather. Extreme events like Hurricane Katrina, which killed 1,830 people in the USA in 2005, are happening more frequently than they used to. Also in the US, in April 2011, around one hundred tornadoes hit six southern states. These resulted in loss of life and damage to property. Record heat waves are also getting more common around the world. In 2010 the temperature in Moscow was very high and forests burned out of control across Russia. In addition, Australia has had extreme summer temperatures with droughts for the last decade.

Elementary level text

'Extreme' weather is when you have a lot of rain, heat or storms and it can be very dangerous. Hurricane Katrina in the USA is an example of extreme weather. The hurricane killed 1,830 people in 2005. Some people think extreme weather is more frequent around the world. For example, in the USA there were around one hundred tornadoes in April 2011. And Australia has had summer droughts for the last 10 years.

10 types of reading comprehension questions

In order to check the students' understanding of a reading text, we often write exercises with about six to eight comprehension questions (though the number will vary, depending on the length of the text). These questions can take different forms. To illustrate the 10 main types of comprehension questions, here is the first part of a longer informational text adapted from an original source for intermediate-level students (see Unit 18). Below it you can read different examples of questions that would check comprehension of this text.

> There's been a change in the weather. Extreme events like Hurricane Katrina, which killed 1,830 people in the USA in 2005, are happening more frequently than they used to. Also in the US, in April 2011, around one hundred tornadoes hit six southern states. These resulted in loss of life and damage to property. Record heat waves are also getting more common around the world. In 2010 the temperature in Moscow was very high and forests burned out of control across Russia. In addition, Australia has had extreme summer temperatures with droughts almost annually for the last decade.

1. *True/False* statements

In this type of exercise, the students are given statements about the information in the text. They have to identify whether these statements are true or false.

1. *The weather today is similar to the weather in the past. True/False*

2. *The tornadoes killed people. True/False*

Answers: 1. False, 2. True

2. Answer *Yes, No* or *Don't know*

This type of exercise has closed questions requiring only a short 'Yes' or 'No' answer. Alternatively, it might ask about information which isn't in the text, so the answer is 'Don't know'. This kind of question encourages the students to read for evidence, rather than assuming the information is in the text.

1. *Does the writer think extreme weather is more common? Yes/No/Don't know*

2. *Does the writer think that humans can stop extreme weather? Yes/No/Don't know*

Answer: 1. Yes, 2. Don't know

3. Open questions

These questions require the students to find a word or phrase in answer to them.

1. *What did the tornadoes cause?*

2. *What are getting more common around the world?*

Answers: 1. Loss of life and damage to property, 2. Heat waves

4. Multiple-choice

This style of question is often used in tests and examinations, as well as in the classroom. The students are given a choice of possible answers.

> In the last 10 years, how often has Australia had droughts?
>
> A Every year
>
> B Most years
>
> C Once in 10 years
>
> Answer: B

5. Note-taking

You can give the students headings and they have to write down any relevant notes related to the heading. For example:

- ▶ *Extreme weather*
- ▶ *Hurricanes and tornadoes*
- ▶ *Extreme heat and drought*

This is an especially useful comprehension task for students who might need to develop note-taking skills.

6. Write in the missing word

This comprehension task asks the students to find a word or phrase from the text and use it to complete a sentence.

> 1. The tornadoes in the southern states resulted in _____.
>
> 2. Australia has had droughts because of _____.
>
> Answers: 1. loss of life and damage to property, 2. extreme summer temperatures

7. Remove sentences

With reading texts, you can remove five or six sentences from the whole text and ask the students to try to work out where these sentences go. Alternatively, you can put gaps in the text and offer three sentences for each one; the students choose the correct sentence. For example:

> Extreme events like Hurricane Katrina, which killed 1,830 people in the USA in 2005, are happening more frequently than they used to. Also in the US, in April 2011, around one hundred tornadoes hit six southern states. (1)____ Record heat waves are also getting more common around the world. In 2010 the temperature in Moscow was very high and forests burned out of control across Russia.

<table>
<tr><td>

(1)

A Heat waves also hit many parts of the world.

B These resulted in loss of life and damage to property.

C There was nothing the people could do about Katrina.

</td></tr>
<tr><td>Answer: (1) B</td></tr>
</table>

8. Gapped text

Sometimes reading texts are given to students with missing words that are gapped. Arguably, this kind of exercise doesn't test understanding of the meaning of the reading, but it can be a useful test of language level. Typically, the gapped words tend to be smaller grammatical or lexical items.

<table>
<tr><td>

Extreme events like Hurricane Katrina, which killed 1,830 people in the USA in 2005, are happening more frequently (1)____ they used to. Also in the US, in April 2011, around one hundred tornadoes hit six southern states. These resulted (2)____ loss of life and damage to property. Record heat waves are also getting more common around the world. In 2010 the temperature in Moscow was very high and forests burned (3)____ of control across Russia.

</td></tr>
<tr><td>Answers: (1) than, (2) in, (3) out</td></tr>
</table>

9. Summarise the paragraph

Write a choice of three sentences. The students have to choose the one which best summarises a paragraph or section of the text.

<table>
<tr><td>

1.

A *The last decade has been difficult for countries like the US and Russia.*

B *Hurricanes and tornadoes are as extreme as heat waves.*

C *The weather is getting more extreme every year.*

</td></tr>
<tr><td>Answer: C</td></tr>
</table>

10. Summarise using key words

Like 9, this next exercise type involves summarising the text, but it is more challenging. You give the students key words from the text. The rubric tells them to cover the reading text, and they must summarise the text using the given words, either orally (to a partner) or by writing a summary. So for the text on weather, the exercise would look like this (though it's important to point out that this type of exercise is usually most effective with longer texts):

<table>
<tr><td>

Work in pairs. Cover the reading text. Summarise the article with your partner using these words:

Extreme weather – Hurricane Katrina – tornadoes – temperatures – fires – droughts

</td></tr>
</table>

ETpedia: Materials Writing © Pavilion Publishing and Media Ltd and its licensors 2017.

Unit 19

10 types of listening text

Before you create listening material for students, you need to consider what they are going to listen to in English in real life and, therefore, what sort of listening they need to practice. If they are planning to travel to an English-speaking country, they may need practice in understanding public announcements and daily conversation; students of EAP may need practice in listening to lectures; business English students may need practice in listening to phone conversations.

Here are 10 types of text, or genre, which can form the basis of a listening exercise.

1. Announcements

The most common announcements that students are likely to encounter are those you might hear in a train station. Other places where announcements are common are airports, planes, shops and stadiums. Listening tasks with announcements often focus on specific details, such as times, dates or instructions.

2. Instructions

Listenings based on instructions often involve listening to a recording of someone explaining how to do something, for example how to cook a particular dish or how to use a computer or phone. The recorded text may take the form of a conversation between two people (one giving instructions to the other) or a set of instructions (as if you were listening to a YouTube how-to video). Listening tasks can involve putting the instructions in order, or actually carrying them out.

3. Telephone conversation

Telephone conversations are another very common text type for listening. The students can either listen to one half of a conversation or both halves. Another variation would be to listen to automated messages, for example voicemail or an automated customer helpdesk service. Listening tasks can involve listening for specific details, or following instructions as in 2 above.

4. News broadcast

This type of listening can be either the newsreader reading out the headlines, or a more in-depth story from a reporter on-site. With this kind of listening, tasks that involve putting events in order or deciding if statements are true or false are common.

5. Audiobook extract

With audiobooks becoming more and more popular, an extract from one could make a good source of listening material. This could be a more descriptive extract, with only one voice reading, or a more dramatic extract from an audiobook with multiple voices and sound effects. Listening tasks will depend in part on the subgenre.

6. A conversation (or dialogue)

This is the most common kind of listening. Conversations should ideally be between two people, three people maximum (if there are more than three, it is hard for the students to distinguish between the voices). Also, if possible, have a male voice and a female voice (again, it can be hard sometimes to distinguish voices in an audio-only version of a

Unit 20

conversation). If you decide to mention the characters by name, make sure the students can readily identify which name goes with which speaker. Conversations can be used for a wide variety of listening tasks, but are commonly used to focus on functional language (eg telling the time, asking for permission, making suggestions, etc.).

7. Lecture or presentation

These two kinds of listening are probably more common in business English or English for academic purposes, but can also appear in general English. More often than not, the text will be an extract from a lecture or presentation, rather than the whole thing, as listenings are rarely more than five minutes long. Listening tasks can involve note-taking and completing graphs or charts.

8. Sports commentaries

Sports commentary is not a text-type commonly used in materials, but it is possible to exploit it for language teaching. Sports commentary has the problem that many names of players will be used; these may not be familiar to the students or may date quickly. One use of sports commentary could be to take several short extracts from different sports and ask the students to identify what sports they are. Other possibilities could include using the chit-chat that often occurs at the beginning of a sports commentary before the event actually begins (about the weather, the crowd, the teams). Listening tasks could involve listening for gist (What sport is being covered?) or specific details (What is the score? Who is winning?).

9. Interviews

Interviews usually come from either radio or television, or more recently from podcasts. It's best to have two very different voices here (preferably a man and a woman). The content of this kind of listening tends to be factual (for example, an interview with an expert) or anecdotal (someone recounting an event that happened to them). Listening tasks will depend in part on what the content is.

10. Game show

This genre of listening often involves some kind of radio or television quiz show. The advantage of this genre is that the listening tasks might not even have to be written separately as they are part of the listening itself (ie the students need to answer the questions in the quiz or game).

"The hardest part about writing is producing interesting texts and audio for skills practice. I prefer to write my own, rather than abridge, and what I like to do is to get an idea from the radio or TV, follow it up in newspapers or magazines, and then use a summary of those ideas to produce a new text at an appropriate level."

Bob McLarty, teacher, author and editor

Unit 20

10 tips on writing and recording your listening dialogues

The previous unit listed some of the many types of listenings that we use in materials. Sometimes you may already have a recording to work with and now you need to write exercises to accompany it (see Unit 22 on writing listening exercises). However, there are also times when you need to write your listening script and then record it. Typically, teachers writing their own materials do so because they need short dialogues which contain useful functional phrases. So if you were writing a dialogue to teach low-level students the kinds of phrases they might need when meeting someone for the first time in a business situation, it might look something like this:

Mary: Hello, are you John?
John: Yes, I am. Are you Susan?
Mary: No, I'm not. I'm Mary. Susan is at the office. Nice to meet you, John.
John: Nice to meet you, too.
Mary: Is this your first time in New York?
John: Yes, it is. I'm very excited to be here.
Mary: We're very excited you're here, too. Welcome to New York!

In this list of tips, you'll find ideas on how to plan and write your dialogue. Tips 6, 7 and 8 suggest ways of making the dialogue sound more natural and authentic, which is especially useful if you want to make the listening more suitable for higher-level material. And the final two tips suggest ways to prepare the dialogue for recording for use in the classroom.

1. Identify the situation

The first thing to do is to identify the situation for your dialogue. This means choosing a situation that feels realistic or at least plausible for the language you want to include. You will want to think of *where* the situation is happening, *who* is speaking, *how many* people there are and *what* is going to happen. Then identify the functional phrases you want to include in the dialogue. Don't force too many in there or it will sound stilted. For more ideas on finding situations that work well with a particular function, refer to a list of functions and suggested situations on page 163 of the appendix.

2. Decide who says what

Write out your dialogue, deciding who says what. For lower levels, you will want to keep this very clear. You'll need at least two people, and with very different voices. At lower levels, the easiest way to achieve this is by having a man and a woman. If you have two men or two women, make sure their voices are different enough to enable the students to distinguish them on a recording.

3. Decide the length of the dialogue

The dialogue length will be important, especially for lower levels. Any dialogue that lasts more than two minutes will become a strain to listen to attentively in class. It may be worth having two or three short dialogues in different situations, rather than one long dialogue. Write the dialogue out first, but then read it back to yourself out loud to ensure it makes sense and sounds natural. By doing this, you will also be able to identify if there are any unnecessary parts.

4. Have something happen

Dialogues that are written to showcase a particular function (eg meeting a person at the airport) can be made more interesting with a little extra detail. You don't need to develop it into a full-blown story, but some detail helps to make it more engaging. Here's an example.

Mary: We're very excited you're here, too. Welcome to New York!

John: Thanks! Oh … wait a second.

Mary: Everything OK?

John: My laptop. I think it's still on the plane!

5. Be careful of distracting language

If you're writing a dialogue to demonstrate functional language, be careful not to include too much distracting language around your target functional phrases. This is especially true at lower levels, where the students will be listening out for those target phrases. Information like times, amounts, money and numbers should be kept simple, unless the purpose of the dialogue is for the students to listen out for that specific information. Finally, give your characters clear and simple names that the students will recognise as names (and that they won't mistakenly think is part of a phrase).

6. Use contractions

Remember that in spoken English contractions are much more common than in formal written English. If you don't use a contraction, the verb will sound more emphasised which, in the absence of context, could make it sound inauthentic. Read the example below out loud with contractions, and then without, to see what we mean.

John: I'm very excited to be here.

Mary: Great. We're excited you're here, too.

7. Add filler sounds and filler words

Sounds like ummm, errr and uhhh are very common in real speech. They are sometimes called 'hesitation devices', as they give the speaker time to think. We also use discourse markers like *so*, *anyway* and *well* a lot in spoken English. If you are writing a dialogue for levels above beginner, sprinkle some of these into your dialogue. Even very low-level students could benefit from hearing one or two. See how the original dialogue above is enhanced by these filler words and sounds.

Mary: Hello, umm, are you John?

John: Yes, I am. Are you Susan?

Mary: Er, no. No, I'm not. I'm Mary. Susan is at the … er … office.

8. Have speakers overlap, and include false starts

It's rare in real-life for speakers to take neat turns, one after another. Often they interrupt and overlap each other. Look how this might happen in our original dialogue.

Mary: Is this your first time in …?

John: Yes, it is. I'm very excited to be here.

Another common feature is a false start. A false start is when we begin to say something, and halfway through it we decide to say something else. Here's an example we could put into our original dialogue.

Mary: No, I'm not. I'm Mary. Susan is … Susan is at the office.

A word of warning about these features. A dialogue devoid of contractions, false starts, overlapping and fillers may sound inauthentic, but the same goes for a dialogue overloaded with them. Don't feel you need to include these elements in every single line.

9. Try it out – and rehearse it

Once you've finished a draft of your dialogue, find a colleague or friend and read it aloud with them. Does it sound OK? The first time you read it out loud, it will be normal to make the odd slip over some of the words or phrases. This doesn't mean it's not right. If on the second or third reading something still sounds wrong, consider changing it.

10. Record it

Current software and hardware make it easier than ever to make a reasonably good quality recording, much better than anything that was possible 10 or 15 years ago. One piece of free and open-source software we have found very useful is Audacity (http://www.audacityteam.org/). Find a quiet place to do your recording, the more enclosed the better (recording in a big open classroom will add echoes, and can make speakers sound as if they're underwater). Stand up while you record, you'll feel more energised. If you are sitting, don't slouch. When you begin recording your dialogue, don't read it too slowly. Work on clear enunciation but at only a slightly slower speed than normal. This applies even to low-level dialogues.

Unit 21

"I like to keep scripts conversational, which generally means sticking to short sentences, phrases, grunts and silences (which can often say more than words). I often write down conversations straight after I've heard them, while they're fresh in my mind. They can become inspiration for stories, especially if they made me chuckle."

Vicki Hollett, materials writer and video creator. Watch her videos at www.simpleenglishvideos.com and YouTube.

10 types of listening comprehension exercise

In the previous two units (20 and 21), we listed different types of listening genre that you might use in your materials and ways of writing and recording your own materials where authentic listening material is not available or not appropriate. Having selected the listening, the materials writer next has to write listening comprehension exercises to accompany it. The following examples begin with listening for gist type exercises and then move on to listening for specific information. Note that in some cases, the exercises and question types are similar to those used for reading comprehension (see Unit 19). However, there are also some comprehension tasks which are better suited to listening and include elements of note-taking.

1. Listen for gist

When writing an exercise that focuses on getting the students to listen for the general meaning or gist, less is more; in other words, the exercise can be a single question. So if we were listening to a short conversation between friends arranging an evening out, we might write the following question:

> **Listen to the conversation. Where do the two friends decide to go for the evening?**

Note that the main answer to this question shouldn't become apparent until towards the end of the listening after the two friends have had some discussion. If they have decided where to go halfway through the conversation, there is no reason for the students to listen to the rest of it.

2. Listen for gist multiple-choice

With more difficult listenings, you might need to guide the students towards understanding the gist. In this case, it can be helpful to give them a choice of possibilities. The example below is a question written to go with an authentic recording that consists of a presentation about modern diets. The fact that it's authentic makes it more challenging, so the writer has created a multiple-choice exercise to narrow down the options for the students:

> **Listen to a presentation. What is the speaker's main aim? Choose from A, B and C.**
>
> A to inform the audience of some facts and figures
>
> B to describe the difference between fresh food and processed food
>
> C to convince the audience to change their eating habits

3. Put the main points in order

Another way to make difficult texts more accessible on the first listening is to provide four or five sentences in the wrong order that sum up what is said in different parts of the recording. In this way, the question gives the students support in terms of what they need to listen out for. Here is an example of a listening question written for a recording of a business meeting.

> **These items are from the agenda of a meeting to plan a conference trip, but they are in the wrong order. Listen to the meeting and number them in the correct order from 1 to 4.**
>
> A Conference schedule
>
> B Any other business
>
> C Hotel bookings
>
> D Update on staffing needs for conference

4. Fill in a table

Listenings that include a lot of factual information, including numerical information and key words, often lend themselves to exercises which target the skill of listening for specific information. One way to structure such an exercise is to provide a table which the students have to fill in while listening. The example below comes from some lesson material where the students listen to a lecture about population growth. They have already listened once and completed an exercise to identify the gist of the lecture. Now they listen again for specific information.

> **Listen to the lecture again. Complete the table with the missing numbers.**
>
> | | In 2000 | 2015 | 2030 |
> |---------|-----------|-----------|-----------|
> | The UK | 58.5m | (1)_____m | 70m |
> | India | (2)_____bn | 1.3bn | (3)_____bn |
> | Brazil | 169m | (4)_____m | 223m |

5. Write notes about key numbers and words

A variation on the previous type of exercise is to provide only the key numbers and words from the listening, and ask the students to make notes about what they refer to. This type of exercise makes the task more challenging, so it's a good way to use the same lecture on global population growth to produce material for higher-level students.

> **Listen for these numbers in the lecture. Write what they refer to.**
>
> a 58.5m_____
>
> b 70m_____
>
> c 1.3bn_____
>
> d 169m_____
>
> e 223m_____

6. Comprehension questions

Many coursebook listening exercises and listening questions in exams are based around fairly standard comprehension questions, many of which you will find suggested for reading comprehension questions in Unit 19. Here are typical question types which have all been written to check comprehension for a listening set in a restaurant:

▶ A closed Yes/No question: *Do they order meat for their main course?*

▶ An open question: *What do they order for their main course?*

▶ Multiple-choice:

They both order _____ for the main course.

A the fish

B the meat

C the salad

7. Controlled note-taking

The skill of note-taking requires the students to be able to listen and write down all the key points themselves. However, we can write listening exercises that help to prepare students to develop this skill gradually. In this first note-taking exercise, the writer has made a set of notes for the listening and then removed certain key words.

Listen to the lecture on how stars are made and read the student's notes. Write in any missing words.

A star is a large _____ of plasma.

In everyday life, the states of matter are solids, liquids, _____ and plasma.

A star is the result of _____ a gas so much that it becomes plasma.

The _____ in our solar system = a _____ and is made of plasma.

Answers: ball, gases, heating, sun, star

---

8. Freer note-taking

You can also write a note-taking exercise so that the students have the keywords in the recording and then add further details. This is a high-level task, but it still provides the students with some guidance. The exercise below is designed for the same recording as in 7.

Listen to the lecture on how stars are made. Write notes about each of these main points:

▶ Definition of a star

▶ How stars are made

▶ The sun

Unit 22

9. Tick the phrase you hear

When using a dialogue to introduce certain useful phrases, there are different ways in which you can structure the accompanying exercise. One useful way is to provide the students with a list of different phrases that could all possibly occur in the listening. This means that even after they have listened and ticked the ones they've actually heard, they have a written reference of other phrases they might use. Here's one such exercise that accompanied a recording of a telephone dialogue to teach phrases for inviting.

Listen and tick the phrases you hear.

Would you like to …? ☐

I was wondering if you'd …? ☐

That'd be great. ☐

Yes, I'd love to. ☐

Thanks for asking, but … ☐

I'm sorry, but I can't … ☐

How about another night? ☐

---

10. Write the phrase you hear

As a more challenging alternative to the exercise in 9, you could give the students a transcript of the dialogue with certain key phrases missing. How much of these phrases you decide to gap will depend on the level of the students and the level of challenge you are aiming at. Here's an exercise for the same recording used in 9, but tailored to higher-level students.

Listen to the telephone conversation and write in the missing words.

A: Hi! It's Josie.

B: Hi, Josie. How are things?

A: Good. Sorry, but I'm calling from work so I need to be quick. (1)_____ if you'd like to go out tonight? To the cinema or something?

B: Oh no! (2)_____ but I'm looking after my younger sister this evening.

A: That's a pity. (3)_____ another night?

Note that writing out the whole dialogue like this can take up a lot of space, so you can also design the exercise so that the students only have the relevant sentences. If you do decide to write the exercise this way, you should always provide some words before the gap begins so that the students can listen out for them and aren't taken by surprise.

---

1. I need to be quick. _____ if you'd like to go out tonight?

2. Oh no! _____ but I'm looking after my younger sister this evening.

3. That's a pity. _____ another night?

---

10 types of speaking exercise

Materials which are used in the face-to-face language classroom usually require speaking exercises and activities. These might form the basis of a whole lesson or they might occur between other stages of the lesson. For example, where a reading text forms the main part of the lesson, you might want to write a short speaking task such as a discussion about the topic or a prediction activity to act as a warmer before the students read the text. On the other hand, a grammar lesson might end with some speaking which practises the target grammar item in the context of other language. In terms of materials creation, it's good to have a variety of speaking exercise types up your sleeve as you'll be writing a lot of them. Here are 10 speaking exercise types as your starting point.

1. Discussion prompts

These usually take the form of questions about the topic of the lesson. It's best to avoid using too many yes/no questions as they will not generate much talk (especially if the answer is 'no'!). If you do include a yes/no question, always have a follow-up question to give the students more to talk about.

Where was the last place you went on holiday?

When is the best time of year to visit your hometown? Why?

Do you think your hometown is a good tourist location? Why or why not?

2. Questionnaire

Questionnaires often ask for a personal response to the topic. Questions can be open or closed, or even have a choice of answers. Sometimes the questionnaire can have an outcome, for example points can be assigned to each answer so that the students calculate their final scores and then read a short explanation of what their score means.

Eating habits questionnaire

How often do you have breakfast? A every morning B only sometimes C never

…

Count the number of As, Bs and Cs you have and read the results. Do you agree?

Mostly As = you are a very healthy eater, well done!

etc.

3. Dialogue

This is often a more restricted speaking activity, but flexibility can be added by giving, for example, one half of a dialogue and asking the students to invent the other half. Alternatively, the students can be asked to create a dialogue in pairs to read out to the class.

ETpedia: Materials Writing © Pavilion Publishing and Media Ltd and its licensors 2017.

Unit 23

Read A's side of the dialogue. Then write what B says. Work in pairs and read the dialogue together.

A: Hi, it's Dominic. How are you?

B:

A: I'm fine, I'm fine. Listen. Are you still free this afternoon?

B:

A: Well, I'd like to meet up and discuss the annual sales convention.

B:

A: How about 4.30? In the meeting room?

4. Role play

Role plays often require more work than a dialogue-reading or dialogue-creation activity and, more importantly, mean that the students have to think on their feet. They need to listen and react to what their partner is saying. See Unit 24 for tips on writing role plays for speaking activities.

5. Information-gap

In an information-gap activity, pairs or groups of students are each given different information. They have to work together to exchange their information in order to complete a task. Typical examples include finding the differences between two pictures or completing a table. Here's an extract from an elementary level information gap where Student A needs to find out the name of the country.

Look at the table below. Ask your partner questions in order to find the missing information.

Student A

Name	From	Job
Lee		Engineer

Student B

Name	From	Job
Lee	United States	Engineer

6. Sentence heads

Sometimes called sentence *stems*, this type of exercise involves providing the students with the beginning of sentences which they must complete and compare with a partner.

Complete these sentences so they are true for you. Then compare your sentences with a partner.

Next year I'm definitely going to …

I might …

I probably won't …

I'm definitely not going to …

---

7. Comparing pictures

Providing two different but related pictures for the students to compare and contrast is a common speaking activity in exams and is popular in teaching materials as well. The images should have something in common, but not be so similar that it's hard to tell them apart. This task is often followed up by a personal question.
For example: Compare and contrast these two photos of problems in a big city.
What are some of the problems facing your home town?

8. Ranking or choosing

You can create a list of items or characteristics and ask the students to work together to put them in order, according to certain specified criteria. Variations include deciding only what the top ones are, or deciding which ones to reject from a list. The discussion can be made longer if you force the students to agree on an order.

Work in pairs. Look at the following places where people sleep. Talk about each place and decide if it is comfortable or uncomfortable. Put them in order from the most comfortable (= 1) to the least comfortable place to sleep (= 6).

a car seat

a hotel room bed

a plane seat

a train sleeping carriage

a sofa

a cabin on a boat

---

9. Anecdotes

This activity involves preparing the students to give a longer individual speaking turn. To get the students to tell a personal anecdote, you will need to create a series of questions to help them generate ideas.

You are going to tell a personal story about a time you were very proud of someone. Think of the answers to these questions.

Who was it?

When did this happen?

Where did this happen?

What did they do that made you so proud?

Were you surprised?

Did you say anything to them?

---

10. Presentations

Classroom presentations are increasingly popular because so many students have to give presentations in English for their academic studies or in their professional work. Normally, it's useful to design the exercise in two stages, with a preparation stage before the stage where the presentation is made to a partner, a group or to the whole class. At a basic level, this kind of exercise can be written in a similar way to the anecdote-type exercise above. In the first part of the exercise, give the students three or four bullet points to help them structure and prepare a short presentation. In the second part, instruct them to give their presentation:

---

1. You are going to give a two-minute presentation about a technological device you can't live without. Structure and prepare your ideas by making notes in answer to these questions:

What is it?

How does it work?

Why can't you live without it?

2. Now work in pairs or groups and give your presentation to the other student(s).

Unit 23

10 tips for writing role plays

Role plays, in which pairs or groups of students are each given a role and asked to improvise a conversation in a given situation, are very good speaking activities, especially for practising functional language (making requests, apologising, going shopping, etc.). You will often find coursebook exercises that involve role play, perhaps with one student looking at a role card on one page and the other turning to a different page to find theirs. The different roles can also be written on cards which are handed out to the students. Whatever the format of your role play, there are some important guidelines to follow when writing them.

1. Less is more

A general rule is to provide the students with just enough information to carry out the role play. Don't overload them with too many details which they have to study and remember. Remember that part of the aim in a role play is that the students should start to add their own ideas to their roles. The text on the role card is essentially to give them the main points that they need to include.

2. Include a name or character

This can be an actual name or just the role eg 'You are Napoleon' or 'You are a graphic designer from New York'. Depending on the level of the students, you can include more or less detail.

3. Include a location

The students need to know where they are. At lower levels, this might mean writing something as straightforward as 'You are in your office' or 'You are in the park'.

4. Include an objective

Good role plays usually have some kind of outcome or desired aim. This can be in the form of a short sentence indicating what the student has to do eg 'Meet as many people as you can at the party' or 'Find a suitable apartment to live in'.

5. Include some useful language

Sometimes it's a good idea to add examples of useful language that the students might need in order to reach their objective. You can suggest a few target expressions for them to use. However, don't overload the role card with too many of these.

6. An odd or even number of students

Where possible, write the role play so that it can work with either an even or an odd number of students. For example, if the role play is one that would normally be used with pairs, think of a way to offer an option for using it with groups of three.

7. Be careful with character emotions

Tip 1 explained that less is more and that you want the students to create the role as well as being told what it is. Adding details about a character's emotions can sometimes be an example of giving students too much information. For example, putting an instruction such as 'You are very angry' can be inhibiting for students unless they are comfortable with acting out emotional situations. A better option is to put details about the situation that will allow these emotions to emerge naturally eg 'It is three o'clock in the morning, and there is still very loud music coming from the street below'.

8. Include roles that are less demanding

If you are writing materials for mixed-ability classes, you could write some roles that will naturally require a little less speaking or thinking time; these are useful for the weaker students in the class and will allow them still to be involved.

9. Role plays related to life experience

For materials which are aimed at students who are learning English for work or perhaps for travel, it makes sense to write role plays which closely resemble the students' real-life needs and experience. If you are designing a telephone role play, for example, the details can match the kind of information a student might talk about in their own work.

10. Fiction and variety

Following on from 9, you might also want to write role plays which are clearly fictional or offer variety. After all, since we often write and use role plays to practise functional language such as arranging to meet or making small talk, it can often make a nice change for the students to use this language in an unusual role play setting. For example, ask them to role-play small talk on a spaceship on its way to Mars. This can add variety, challenge and fun to the material. See page 164 in the appendix for 10 ideas for different kinds of role play to give you an idea of the range of situations that are possible.

Unit 24

"When I write materials for young learners, I keep role plays short, simple and easy. They have to generate the target language and be adaptable for a mixed ability classroom. I also like to add a fun language chunk like 'goodness gracious me, that's enough' or 'what a nutty idea!' in the role play which the children will remember and apply to other contexts long after the activity is over!"

Vanessa Reis Esteves, teacher and author of ETpedia Young Learners

10 types of writing exercises

The types of writing exercises you will write and set for your students will often depend on the type of examination they are preparing for or the type of writing they may need to do in their professional or academic lives. These types of writing can be broadly categorised into three types:

- ▶ discursive/academic writing: *for and against essays, articles giving an opinion, etc.*
- ▶ correspondence/professional writing: *letters, emails, short reports, etc.*
- ▶ fictional and descriptive writing: *short stories, news articles, people and places, etc.*

There are different ways to write exercises for all of these and if you are writing exam practice exercises, you will need to simulate the style of the questions in the exam. 1 to 4 below are examples of how you might write a question for discursive writing. Example 4 is also useful for students who need to write for their working lives, and 5 to 7 are also aimed at this type of student. The final three examples are suggestions for ways to write exercises for stories and descriptive writing.

1. A *for* and *against* question

This is a popular type of question in exams. It gives the students a topic to discuss. The topic shouldn't require any specialist knowledge, and the students have to be able to think of some points for and against, before giving their own view at the end. Make sure when writing this type of question that you choose a topic that all the students are likely to know something about.

> **Write an essay discussing both these views and give your own opinion.**
> Some people believe social media is an effective way to communicate news and information, and bring people together. However, others feel it contributes to social problems such as bullying and stress-related illnesses.

2. Giving an opinion on a statement

Unlike the previous question, the next example gives the students less guidance on the structure of the writing. The focus is on them giving their opinions and providing supporting reasons. Again, the question needs to be on a topic which the students can easily come up with ideas on – otherwise, there's a danger that they will lose marks for lack of subject knowledge, rather than being judged on their language use.

> **Students should be allowed to choose all the subjects they study in school. Do you agree?**

3. Giving an opinion with prompts

For lower levels, you can write questions which also provide the students with a framework to structure their writing. Try to keep the prompts as brief as possible so they are easy to understand. Avoid long complex sentences in the instructions as this will make it a reading task rather than a writing task:

> **In the future, more people will work from home than travel to work. Do you agree?**
> **Write about the following points in your essay:**
> Commuting time to work
> Internet access and online communication
> Your own idea

Unit 25

4. Providing visual information

Examination such as IELTS and materials designed for professional or academic English often include exercises where the students need to interpret graphs, charts or tables and integrate the information into their answer to the question. Here is an example of the sort of exercise you might write. Note that it's worth looking out for any kind of visual information on recent research in a newspaper or creating your own graphs and charts based on recent findings in a survey.

The charts below show the results of a survey in the USA into online gaming. Summarise the main information in each chart and discuss the findings, including your opinions on online gaming.

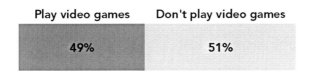

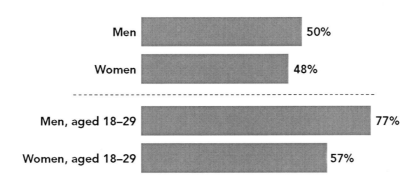

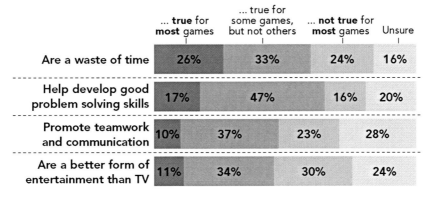

Source for all three is http://www.pewinternet.org/2015/12/15/gaming-and-gamers/

Unit 25

5. Provide a reason to respond

For writing exercises that involve correspondence and transactional communication, provide the students with an email (or letter) similar to the example below. Make sure that the level of the English in the question doesn't challenge them too much: the aim is not to test their reading level but to get them to produce a piece of writing. The content also needs to demand a response from the student, so it needs to provoke in some way or even ask questions that need answering.

Your customer service department receives this email from a customer.

Dear Sir or Madam,

I would like to complaint about the service I recently received at your branch in Oxford.
On Saturday 10th at 10am I stood in a line of customers and waited 30 minutes to purchase some items of clothing. When I finally reached the counter, the sales assistant offered no apology. In addition, I had a question about how to wash the wool sweater and the assistant was unable to advise me. In total, it took me an hour to purchase the goods, which I think is unacceptable.

Write a reply (about 120 words) and give reasons for the difficulties.

---

6. Prompts for an email

This next example is to get the students to write a short email. It is designed for lower-level students who need to learn how to write basic correspondence. It's useful to use bullet points, as shown in this example, as they provide the students with a structure to follow and the key points to include in their writing. It also allows you to mark it more easily because you can check that they have included each point.

You are organising a training day for 10 employees. Write an email to your assistant with the following points:

confirm the room number and the date

ask your assistant if the participants have completed the pre-course questionnaire

also ask the assistant to contact catering about providing lunch, tea and coffee during the day

---

7. The structure of a report

This is an example of where the materials writer guides the students towards structuring their writing in a certain way. The task is to write a report, and the instructions tell the students to organise their response by first writing about each of the three options given and then writing a recommendation. Note that this kind of exercise is based around a topic where the students can use their own general knowledge, so it isn't testing any kind of specialist background knowledge:

A local council has some money to invest in a local community facility. They have asked you to consider three different types of facility, report on each one, and make a final recommendation. Here are the three options: a swimming pool, a small theatre or a library.

---

8. Sentences in a story

If you are creating an exercise in which the students are going to write a story, you might give them just the title of the story and ask them to start writing. However, a good alternative is to provide a sentence that must appear in the story. Here are two examples of rubrics which provide the sentences to appear at the beginning and end of a story:

> **Write a story of between 140 to 190 words starting with the sentence: I'd left my house in a hurry that morning and forgotten to lock the front door.**

> **Write a story of between 140 to 190 words ending with the sentence: After everything that had happened on the journey, it was a relief to see my friends waiting on the platform.**

9. Prompts for a story

Like the example of an email writing task in 6, bullet-point prompts can also direct the students to include certain language, and also provide some structure to their writing. Here is an example of how this might be done for a story.

> **Write a story about your first day at school. Your story must include:**
>
> a particular school subject
>
> a surprise

10. Create a context to respond to

In this question, the writer wants the students to produce a piece of descriptive writing. As with some of the earlier examples in this unit, the question is designed around the idea of creating a context which demands a response. In this case, it takes the form of an advert:

> **You have seen this announcement in a student magazine. Write your description.**
>
> # Travel story competition!
>
> **This month we have a story competition. Write a description of something that happened to you on your summer holidays.**
>
> **The winner will receive a £20 book token.**

Unit 25

10 exercises for practising writing subskills

Exercises for developing the students' writing skills may require them to produce complete texts (see Unit 25), or the focus may be on practising the subskills of writing, such as paragraphing or using linking words, correct punctuation and discourse markers, etc. These exercises will practise writing at the word and sentence level, as well as encouraging the students to notice how different texts are structured. Here are 10 of the most common areas that are practised in subskills materials.

1. Conjunctions and linking words

We teach students to join sentences together with linking words so that their writing will become more sophisticated. One simple way to write an exercise to practise this is to give the students two separate sentences and ask them to choose an appropriate conjunction or linking word to join them together. Here is an example from some lower-level material:

Join the two sentences using the conjunctions *and*, *so* or *but*.

1. *I live in London. I work for an IT company.*

2. *I live in London. I was born in Paris.*

3. *I live in London. I can often go out to the theatre.*

Answers:
1. *I live in London and I work for an IT company.*
2. *I live in London but I was born in Paris.*
3. *I live in London so I can often go out to the theatre.*

---

2. Capital letters and punctuation

Choose a sentence or extract from a text and remove all the punctuation. Ask the students to rewrite it, putting in capital letters and correct punctuation. For example:

Rewrite the sentence with the correct capital letters and punctuation.

every year different cities around the world such as rio de janeiro in brazil and new orleans in the usa celebrate the festival of mardi gras

Answer: *Every year, different cities around the world, such as Rio de Janeiro in Brazil and New Orleans in the USA, celebrate the festival of Mardi Gras.*

---

3. Paragraphs

Many students don't make use of paragraphs when writing essays. One simple way to encourage them is to take a model version of an essay, perhaps with five paragraphs, and edit it so there are no paragraphs and it appears as a solid block of text. Give the students the following rubric:

This essay should have five separate paragraphs. Find the beginning and end of each paragraph and circle it.

4. Topic sentences and supporting sentences

Showing students how to structure an individual paragraph is also important, especially if they have to write for examinations such as the Cambridge First, the Cambridge Advanced or IELTS. To introduce this idea, a re-ordering exercise like this one is helpful:

Read four sentences from a paragraph and number them in the correct order (from 1 to 4) with the topic sentence first and then the three supporting sentences.

a) In addition, employers can reduce the cost of office space. ___

b) In the last decade, the internet and digital communication have had a major impact on the way we work. ___

c) For example, many employees are able to work remotely: they don't always need to go to an office but can log on from home. ___

d) This allows greater flexibility for the employee and reduces the amount of time spent travelling. ___

Answer: 1b), 2c), 3d), 4a)

---

5. Cohesion and reference words

Students need to learn how to use certain types of words that add cohesion to a text. Typically, these are pronouns. It's useful to take a text with a range of pronouns in it and ask the students to identify them and say what they refer to. Here is an example of such an exercise:

Read the paragraph and answer these questions.

Sentence 1: Who does 'we' refer to?

Sentence 2: Who does 'they' refer to?

Sentence 3: What does 'This' refer to?

In the last decade, the internet and digital communication have had a major impact on the way we work. For example, many employees are able to work remotely: they don't always need to go to an office, but can log on from home. This allows greater flexibility for the employee and reduces the amount of time spent travelling. In addition, employers can reduce their overheads.

Answers: 1. everyone, including the reader, 2. employees, 3. the fact that they don't need to go to an office and can log on from home

---

Unit 26

6. Abbreviations

Certain text types, such as official forms, business correspondence and reports, are likely to include abbreviations, which the students may need to be familiar with and may have to use in their own writing. A simple exercise is to write these out in full and have the students find examples in the text. This example comes from an exercise where the students read a formal letter.

Find the abbreviations in this letter which mean:

1. road _____

2. doctor _____

3. with reference to _____

4. enclosed with the letter _____

Answers: 1. Rd. 2. Dr. 3. Ref. 4. encs.

---

7. Formal and informal language

Students need to be able to shift the register of their writing. One way to introduce the idea of register in language is to devise a simple matching exercise like the one below. Alternatively, if you have a text written in formal language, the students can be given several informal words and asked to find the equivalent formal words in the text. You can also give the students a text written informally and ask them to rewrite it formally.

Match the less formal words on the left with the formal words on the right.

1. ask for	a) apologise
2. say sorry	b) delighted
3. tell	c) request
4. happy	d) inform

Answers: 1. c), 2. a), 3. d), 4. b)

---

8. Noticing useful expressions

When you want the students to write certain text types which contain high frequency language, it's a good idea to take a model text and ask them to underline the key language. For example, this exercise comes from a set of materials aimed at students who are going to write academic English.

> **Read the text and underline any useful words or expressions for writing about cause and effect.**
>
> *For the first time ever, more people are living in the city than in the countryside. As a result, there is greater pollution in city centres and, because of this, rates of ill-health are on the increase ...*
>
> Answers: As a result / because of this

9. Applying useful expressions

Once the students have identified useful expressions in a text, they will need an exercise in which they can apply the new language they have noticed. So for the language of cause and effect (see 8 above), you could follow up with an activity like this:

> **Connect these causes and effects using some of the expressions you discovered in the text.**
>
> 1. more people drive cars > pollution is increasing
>
> 2. young people are moving to the cities > traditional life in the countryside is disappearing
>
> 3. more people eat processed food nowadays > rates of obesity are increasing
>
> Possible answers:
> 1. More people drive cars. As a result, pollution is increasing.
> 2. Young people are moving to the cities, so traditional life in the countryside is disappearing.
> 3. More people eat processed food nowadays. Because of this, rates of obesity are increasing.

10. Summarising

After the students have read a long text, having them summarise it is a useful activity. It develops the skill of selecting key words in a text and restating them. This is a skill which is often required for academic writing. One way to help the students to develop this skill is to identify the keywords from the text and ask the students to summarise the text using these words, within a set word limit. The rubric might be:

Write a summary of the article using 80–100 words. Use these 10 words and phrases from the article in your summary.

Writing complete lessons and worksheets

If you have chosen to read the sections in this book in order, then you'll be aware how the units have moved from writing basic question types and exercises for language practice to developing texts with comprehension questions and writing freer practice activities. This section starts to bring all these different areas into materials for complete lessons which are built on a series of exercises which flow from one into the next.

This section also looks at the issue of writing materials for other teachers to use. So, for example, if you write a worksheet which your colleagues might also want to use, you will need to make sure it's clear to them how to use it. One key factor here is the effective writing of rubrics: the instructions that explain what to do in an exercise.

You'll also find ideas on how to develop your materials by making use of design features and images.

10 tips on writing complete lessons and worksheets

In the first half of this book, many of the units look at materials writing in terms of writing separate exercises. This is especially helpful when you are writing self-study materials, single practice exercises to supplement other materials such as a coursebook, or for test writing. However, if you are writing materials to be used in a complete classroom lesson, there are new considerations. This type of material often takes the form of a one- or two-page worksheet and resembles the type of content you might see on the page of a coursebook or download as a pdf or Word document from a website.

Many of the tips presented in Unit 9 on writing a controlled practice exercise (see page 37) also apply to this kind of writing. The 10 tips that follow build on those ideas and present new considerations when planning and writing a complete lesson in the form of a worksheet. When reading these tips, refer to the example of a worksheet with teacher's notes in the appendix on pages 166–169, which is provided to illustrate the typical features of a worksheet.

1. Give your worksheet or lesson a title

A title at the top of the worksheet helps the teacher and the student start thinking what the lesson is going to be about. A title is also helpful as a reference tool when a teacher is filing or saving the worksheet; the students will also find a title useful when they discover the paper in their bag at a later date or are looking for a particular worksheet to revise from. When choosing a title, you can use something witty or interesting, but as a general rule it is a good idea to try to include words that indicate the topic of the lesson, especially for lower-level materials. So, if you were going to base a lesson around a reading on the theatre, you might call the lesson 'All the world's a stage' at higher levels, but for lower levels, a simple title like 'At the theatre' might be more useful.

2. List of aims

Some worksheets include a list of bullet points at the top of the page to indicate what the main aims of the lesson are. Again, this is helpful for teachers and students to refer to and provides an outline of what the lesson includes. So a worksheet about asking for and giving directions might have a list like this:

▶ Vocabulary: Places in the city

▶ Listening: Following directions on a map

▶ Speaking: Asking for and giving directions

3. Exercise 1

The first exercise is your lead-in and is the moment when the teacher has to engage the students in the lesson. Usually this exercise will involve the students speaking about the topic. See Unit 31 for 10 ideas on writing lead-in exercises.

4. Images

Having an image at the top of a worksheet is much more visually interesting than just presenting the students with a page of text. Sometimes you can use a picture purely to enhance the design, but ideally you will want to integrate it into an exercise, such as a lead-in, or use it as part of the main task. See Unit 32 for 10 ways to use images in your materials.

5. The flow of the exercises

What really separates writing a single exercise from a worksheet is that you are bringing together a series of exercises which must flow naturally into each other. Your worksheet might, for example, take a present–practice–produce approach, where the first two or three exercises present new language; then the students do some controlled practice exercises; and finally they do a productive task such as a discussion activity. With a reading skills lesson worksheet, the first exercise might consist of prediction questions about the reading, followed by two reading comprehension tasks, then a vocabulary exercise, ending with a summary-writing exercise. How you structure the worksheet depends on your methodology or the methodology of the teachers you are writing it for.

6. Ensure variety from one exercise to the next

Check that each exercise is sufficiently different from the one before and the one after. If you have two controlled practice gap-fill exercises in a row, you might want to think about changing one of them into an ordering exercise or a matching exercise. Another technique to ensure variety is to apply the heads-up/heads-down rule: having some exercises where the students' heads are up and communicating with each other and/or the teacher, and some where they are down, looking at the worksheet. Typically, a heads-up exercise is used at the start of the lesson and during productive speaking tasks. A heads-down exercise needs the students to be looking at the worksheet and may involve filling in gaps or reading a text. The idea of describing exercises and tasks as 'heads-up' and 'heads-down' is useful because it helps a writer to picture how the materials will flow in a lesson. As a general rule, a series of exercises on a worksheet flow if there is a good combination of exercises with the students' heads up looking at each other, and exercises which require the students' heads to be down looking at the material.

7. Navigational tools

'Navigational tools' refer to anything on the page which helps the teacher and students to find their way around the material. So titles and sub-headings are part of this but also rubrics (see Units 29–30) and numbering (see page 140) are the basic tools which help a teacher to manage the material quickly.

8. Language reference boxes

If you want to teach language items such as a key set of vocabulary, functional expressions or a grammar point, it's helpful to sum up the form, use and meaning of the language in a titled box. That way, it's easy for the students to refer to and they always know where to find the 'rule'. (See also Unit 40.)

9. The final exercise

Usually, the final task in a lesson is productive, authentic in some way, and offers the chance for the students to personalise the language. It's normally a heads-up task (though not necessarily – in a writing lesson, for example). It will also be a task that allows the teacher to monitor and take note of what the students have learnt in the lesson and what they still need to work on. Typically, it will involve extended speaking, so you'll need to scaffold the stages of the exercise carefully.

Unit 27

10. 'Can do' checklists

In recent years, it has become popular to end a set of lesson materials or a unit in a coursebook with a checklist of points covered. The idea is that the students review these points at the end and say if they think they can now do them as a result of having worked through the material. For example:

I can talk about different places in a city. ☐

I can listen to someone describing directions on a map and follow them. ☐

I can ask for and give directions. ☐

> "When writing effective worksheets and lesson materials, ask yourself: Does the lesson flow, does it make a whole, or is it just a pile of disconnected Lego bricks? Is there a clear path through the lesson? Are the transitions smooth? Does the material carry the learners along so that each stage feels like a natural progression from the last?"
>
> **Rachael Roberts, ELT author, UK**

Unit 27

10 starting points for planning your lesson material

In Unit 27, there were tips on writing worksheets which focused on the structure and organisation of a worksheet. Of course, you also need to start somewhere in terms of the language that is to be taught. So, when you are faced with a blank page that you need to fill with material, where do you start? You may have an idea of what the material will be, or a list of things from your syllabus that have to be included, but the point of departure may be different, depending on what area you are going to focus on. It also helps to have a range of starting points for a piece of material – if you get stuck trying to start from one angle, try a different one. Below are 10 different starting points for any complete lesson's worth of material you might be creating.

1. Language point

This is usually the first point of departure. Think of the language point that you want or need to present (grammar, vocabulary or both) and brainstorm contexts and exercises that go with that language point. This is one of the most traditional ways of going about materials creation.

2. Topic or idea

Another common way is to begin with a topic (eg sports, Valentine's Day, movies) and think of exercises that would go well with that topic.

3. Final outcome

This is beginning with the ending. Think of what the learners are going to achieve by the end of the lesson and work your way backwards. What language and skills will they need in order to accomplish this outcome?

4. A difficulty

Think about the language you are going to teach via this material. What are the common problems that learners have with this language? Start by brainstorming exercise types and examples that help address those problems first.

5. A text

Materials writers are constantly on the lookout for interesting texts and often have a collection of them. Using a suitable and interesting text (authentic or adapted) as a starting point should also help provide context for subsequent practice exercises.

6. Audio or video

As with choosing a written text in 5 above, you may want to start with a piece of audio or video that will engage the students and which includes lots of useful language. Then you build a set of exercises around the content.

7. An exercise type

If you are writing material that requires the students to practise a certain type of exercise, it may be worth using that as your starting point. This is particularly true if you are writing material to prepare the students for exams.

Unit 28

8. A skill or subskill

If your material is focused on one or more of the four skills, you could start by thinking of a subskill that the students can usefully practise. Choosing this first will determine what kind of text input you will use, as you'll want to choose one which lends itself easily to practising that subskill.

9. Work-based English

If you are developing lesson materials for students who need English for their job, then a good starting point is to take material that they use in their work and build exercises around it; for example, if your student receives certain types of emails in English (ie emails to place orders), refer to these when creating an authentic context for the material.

10. Existing material

All effective writers are aware of what has gone before them and the type of materials that other people have written. So when starting on a piece of material, it can be useful to look at what others have already done. This doesn't mean copying, but looking at how others have tackled types of lessons or language points. This process can provide much needed inspiration on how to produce your own.

"When I start planning my material, I look for a text (reading or listening) which includes an 'Oh, I didn't know that!' element. So I spend ages researching a topic, and trying to find a good angle. Throughout all this I have to keep the target language in mind, and incorporate it as naturally as possible. Once I've got a near-final draft, I get someone who's not a language teacher to read it, and if they can't spot the target language, then that's good! And then I start working with the language and exercises."

Rachel Appleby, teacher and writer, Budapest

Unit 28

10 common types of rubrics

Rubrics, also called 'direction lines' in the USA, are the instructions that appear at the beginning of an exercise. They tell the teacher and the students what they have to do in order to complete the task. Often, when teachers write their own materials for a lesson, they omit the rubric. This is because they already know how they are going to use the material and how they expect their students to complete the exercise. However, if the students are going to complete exercises for self-study, without the guidance of a teacher, they need clear instructions to follow. Also, if you expect that the material will be used by other teachers, they will need rubrics to follow. Here are 10 of the most commonly used rubrics to illustrate the different reasons why they are important.

1. 'Answer questions 1 to 8.'

The most basic function of the rubric is to tell the students what to do. Remember that for the students the whole task, including the rubric, is in a foreign language. It's important to spell things out clearly and simply.

2. 'Match 1–7 to a–f.'

This rubric might go with an exercise where the students have to match two halves of a set of sentences. Using numbers and letters in both the rubric and to denote the parts of the exercise makes referencing easy so that teachers can check the answers as a class without confusion. It also makes it easy to produce an answer key so that the students can quickly check their own answers.

3. 'You are going to watch a video about …'

Some rubrics tell the students what is going to happen next and help to set up the context. For example, if they are going to watch a video, it's useful for them to know something about the content. Similarly, you could use the same rubric for reading or listening activities: eg 'You are going to read/listen to a text about …'.

4. 'Work in pairs.'

This type of rubric explains how to set up interaction in the classroom. The same rubric can be written as 'Work with a partner' and for groupwork you'll write something like 'Work in small groups'.

5. 'See the example below.'

Many exercises include an example, so the rubric might read 'See the example' or 'For example:'. Then the first question in the exercise is filled in so as to show the students clearly what is expected. For speaking exercises, it's also helpful to include an example sentence of the type of thing that the students might say or to show how they might begin a discussion.

6. 'What do you think about the opinion in the article? Tell your partner.'

Sometimes we embed one or two discussion questions in the rubric. Generally, this type of task comes between two longer exercises and offers a chance for some heads-up speaking or sharing of ideas.

Unit 29

7. 'Read the grammar summary on page 100.'

Rubrics are all about navigating the teacher and students through the material, so often they will send the user forward or backward to another part of the book or to something on the same page. For example, *'Look back at the sentences in Exercise 5 and underline any verbs in the present perfect'*.

8. 'Student A: You are the customer. Student B: You are the shop assistant.'

We often use rubrics which call the students A and B, sometimes even C and D, for pairwork or groupwork which will involve them having different roles or carrying out different tasks. Writing simple rubrics for more extended and complex tasks like this is notoriously difficult. Calling the students A, B, C or D is often the most effective way to explain what they each have to do.

9. 'You have two minutes.'

In order to set time limits and create a bit of pressure, your rubric might refer to the length of time available for the activity. This is especially useful for an activity that is open-ended, such as a speaking or discussion task. It's also good for anything competitive and lets the teacher know they need to time the task.

10. 'Present your ideas to the rest of the class.'

This is a classic one-line rubric that often comes at the end of a worksheet or a lesson in a book. Having had the students discuss an issue in groups, you now want each group to present their ideas and compare their thoughts with the rest of the class. It's also a chance for the teacher to listen and make notes on language use in a free practice stage before giving final feedback.

"Rubrics are the signposts, the scaffolding that holds the material together, and helps make sense of it."

Ceri Jones, teacher and coursebook author

10 tips on writing effective rubrics

Writing badly worded and confusing rubrics is easily done. They can become too long, vague, and written in a way that becomes more difficult to understand for the student than the exercise they are expected to complete. Here are 10 tips that will help you write rubrics quickly and effectively.

1. Be consistent

Certain types of rubric will be repeated throughout your material, so be consistent and repeat them. In other words, if you write 'Work in pairs' in one exercise, try to use the same rubric in later exercises rather than changing it to 'Work with another student' or 'Find a partner'. That way, the students will become used to what is being asked and not spend unnecessary time trying to understand the rubric.

2. One action per sentence

As a general rule, each sentence of your rubric should include one action – at least, no more than two. So 'Work in pairs' is one action. 'Work in pairs and ask each the questions below' is safe because both actions are simple. However, a rubric like 'Work in pairs, ask each other the questions below and try to use all the words in the previous exercise' suddenly becomes confusing.

3. Imperatives in rubrics

Rubrics written for in-class materials are usually aimed at students and teachers so, typically, we write rubrics using imperative forms such as 'Answer the questions', 'Read the article', 'Listen to the interview'. This style of writing is quick and easy for the students to understand. For certain types of tasks and at higher levels, you might vary this approach, but as a general guideline, imperative forms work well.

4. Personalising the rubric

You might vary the approach in tip 3 above when writing for students who are using self-study materials without a teacher. Rubrics with this kind of material often include 'You' a lot more in the rubric to give a more personal and supportive 'voice'. For example, 'When you have finished the questions, you can check your answers on page 000'. You might also use this kind of approach to rubrics when writing instructions for a teacher in a set of teacher's notes (see Unit 42).

5. Avoid too many clauses

Following on from 2, a rubric with too many additional clauses is often an indication that it's too complex. So a rubric like 'Answer the questions below and then ask your partner any of the questions below which you think are useful to you' includes a conjunction and a relative clause, and probably needs to be broken down into two separate sentences.

6. Shorter than the exercise

If you want your students to complete an eight-line exercise but your rubric is longer than that, it's clearly unnecessarily long!

ETpedia: Materials Writing © Pavilion Publishing and Media Ltd and its licensors 2017.

7. Lower than the students' level

If you are writing material for students at a pre-intermediate (A2) level, then the rubric needs to be written at a level which will not present a challenge at that language level. Rubrics are not there to test the students' level but to move them quickly onto the main exercise.

8. No more than three

In general, clear rubrics tend to consist of one or two sentences. You might need to use three sentences for exercises such as role play tasks or groupwork where the task is complex. Here's an example of such a rubric: *Work in groups of three. Plan a holiday using the items in Exercise 4. Discuss what you need to take and why.*

9. When to create new rubrics

Following on from the tip in 8, if you have four sentences in your rubric, this suggests that the exercise needs to be broken down into more stages, with a new rubric for each one. For example, this rubric is too long because it is introducing too many stages at once: *Work in groups of three. Plan a holiday using the items in Exercise 4. Discuss what you need to take and why. Then present your ideas to another group and compare them.*

In this case, it would be better to introduce the final sentence in the rubric as a separate numbered exercise.

10. Pilot the rubric

When writing complex rubrics, always test your instructions by giving them to another teacher (or editor). By reading your rubric, they should clearly understand what is expected.

"One common mistake that I've found new authors make is to replicate the voice of the teacher [in their rubrics]. So they might say: 'Now, it's not easy, but where do you think the photo was taken ... go on ... have a guess!".

Ben Goldstein, ELT author and teacher trainer

10 types of lead-in exercise

Most teachers are familiar with the need to have a good lead-in for any lesson. It's all about finding a way of taking even the dullest-sounding topic and making it interesting and engaging for any kind of learner. When we write materials, we have to make this work on the page and provide a way into the lesson which will make the class want to move from Exercise 1 to Exercise 2. Note that the following 10 ideas for opening exercises could, of course, be used later in the lesson or even at the end. However, they naturally make good beginnings.

1. Lead-in questions

Writing an exercise that begins with the rubric *Discuss the questions below* (or similar variations such as *Discuss these questions in pairs*, etc.) is probably the most popular way to start a worksheet or a page in a coursebook. The questions are a way to get the students thinking about the topic of the lesson, and they also help the teacher to establish what the students already know (both in terms of content knowledge and language knowledge).

Typically, there will be two or three questions. The first question in a lesson about sport could be a Yes/No closed question such as '*Do you often play sport?*'. The second question will naturally be more open – for example, '*What kinds of sports do you like?*' – followed by an extension question: '*Why do you like them?*'. Note that these opening questions are often aimed at eliciting personal responses, even at lower levels. In higher-level materials, the questions are often broader and demand more complex responses. So for materials for a lesson about sport for intermediate levels and above, the questions could be '*Some people believe that sport in schools is too competitive. Why do you think they say this? Do you agree?*'

2. A picture

An interesting or striking picture at the beginning of your materials can serve the purpose of setting the theme of the lesson and engaging the students. You can also set questions about it with a rubric like:

> 1. Look at the photo. What is the man doing? Why do you think he is running?

(See also Unit 32 on using pictures in materials.)

3. A questionnaire or survey

This is an extension to the idea of starting the material with questions. You give the students a short questionnaire. They can work in pairs, ask each other the questions and fill in the questionnaire for their partner. Quite often, materials writers find these types of questionnaires in lifestyle magazines or surveys that were done online. (See Unit 36 on writing questionnaires.)

4. A video

With a video lesson, one exercise that works well at the beginning is to play the first 10 seconds of the video and ask the students to say what they saw and to predict what the whole video is about or what might happen. (See Unit 38 on writing video materials.)

5. Sound effects

As with video, playing three or four sound effects that connect with the lesson in some way lends itself to getting the students to say what they think the lesson might be about. This is especially useful as a lead-in to material which is teaching the language of fiction and stories. You will find many different sound effects to choose from on these websites: SoundBible.com and Freesound.org.

6. Ranking

Getting the students to work together to rank a list of items in order is another good exercise to start a lesson because it is interactive and generates discussion early on. Here's a typical rubric for this type of exercise from a lesson with the theme of 'inventions':

---

1. Look at this list of inventions and put them in order of importance (1 = most important, 7 = least important).

computer   aeroplane   solar power   bicycle   vacuum cleaner   book washing machine

2. Compare your list with a partner and try to agree.

---

7. A quote

Some materials begin with a quote by a famous person for the students to discuss. Here is an example from a worksheet for business English learners on the topic of success:

---

1. Read this quote. Do you agree with Colin Powell? Why? What else do you think success is the result of?

'There are no secrets to success. It is the result of preparation, hard work, and learning from failure.' Colin Powell

---

8. Predict the connection

For lessons which will involve long reading or listening texts, you can choose some interesting words that appear in the text and use them in the opening exercise, like this:

---

1. These words are from the reading text. Work in pairs and discuss what you think the connection is between them. Afterwards, tell the class your ideas.

Brooklyn Bridge   85mph   a dog   two cats   the police   builders   sunglasses the Mayor of New York

---

9. A quiz

Quizzes can be motivating ways to start a lesson. For example, if the topic of the lesson is history, the quiz could test general knowledge, with the students working in groups to decide on the answers. Exercises can also be 'quizlike', where the students have to guess something. If you are writing materials which require the students to use plenty of new vocabulary, you could activate some of it in the first exercise. Here's an example from a unit on sport in which students work with sports vocabulary:

---

1. Work in groups of three. List the names of different sports that use this equipment:
gloves, a net, a shuttlecock, a puck, a racquet, skates, water

Afterwards, compare your lists with the rest of the class. Which group listed the most correct sports?

---

10. 'Work on your own' exercises

The previous nine exercises have all been examples of lead-in exercises to introduce the material; they all involved some kind of speaking, which, as a general rule, is a good way into the lesson. However, from time to time, it is good to start the lesson with the students working alone and maybe reading a short text or even writing something down. This is especially true if you are writing a series of materials which will be used one after the other (ie for a coursebook) and you want to add some variety or a change of pace now and again.

"A good lead-in activity is a bit like a good advertisement. It must immediately engage the student, focus attention on the topic, and stimulate interest in what is to come, without pre-empting it too much."

Paul Dummett, teacher and coursebook author

Unit 31

10 tips on using images in lesson materials

Images in material can serve a cosmetic or teaching purpose. Using an image for cosmetic purposes means that it is there purely as decoration for the material, to help make it look more attractive and inviting to the students: there may not be anything you actually *do* with the image. Images play an important part in helping 'lift' material off the page.

However, of more interest to the materials writer is using images for teaching purposes. In this unit, we explore the use of images in material – and look at what kind of images might work best. (Note that when using other people's images, you will always need to check the copyright situation; see Unit 47 on copyright and permissions.)

1. To teach vocabulary

The most common use of an image is to teach the vocabulary for a specific thing. Sometimes this means using lots of little photos, illustrations or clipart, with one image for each word or phrase. At other times it could mean using one image with lots of things in it to achieve the same result.

2. To make the topic clear

You can make the topic or theme of your material much clearer with a photograph. For example, if you have a lesson on sports, you could have various photos of people doing different sports. If you have a lesson with a focus on meeting people in business situations, then a few photos of different business meetings would help.

3. To set the mood

If you want to convey a mood in the material, use images to help. For example, a piece of material about Britain in the 1960s might have some news photos of the time (or headlines) dotted around, even if they are not explicitly taught.

4. As a lead-in

A photo, painting or other kind of image can be a very effective way of leading into a lesson (see Unit 31). If you are using an image in this way, make sure it's big enough for the students to see and that any work you want to do with it won't be undermined by anything else that the students can see on the page. For example, if you have a picture of a shark and the question 'Where do you think this photo was taken?' and on the same page there is a text with a big title 'Giant shark found off the south coast of Australia', then you need to rethink.

5. For speaking activities

After teaching vocabulary, the most common use for an image is to act as support or inspiration for speaking activities. At its most simple, this can involve the students describing or talking about a photograph. Having two illustrations of the same thing with minor differences can be used for information-gap pairwork activities. A series of images can be used for more creative speaking activities as well, for example telling a story using the pictures (or a dream, or a fantasy vacation …). Paintings can be a good source of material for these kinds of activities.

6. For writing activities

Many of the uses of an image for a speaking activity can also be applied to a writing activity. Other writing activities that make use of images include writing headlines for news photos, or captions for cartoons. Taking a comic strip and removing the text from the speech bubbles also creates a potential writing activity.

7. To clarify language

Another kind of image is a more technical one, such as a chart of some kind or a graph. Charts and graphs can be very helpful in illustrating a grammar point (eg a graph showing adverbs of frequency) or vocabulary (eg a chart showing the various forms words can take). Charts and graphs can also be an integral part of practice exercises, with the students completing missing parts of them.

8. To clarify a text or as a text in itself

English for specific purposes (such as business English) or for academic purposes often makes use of images. These are commonly diagrams, which can support texts, especially texts that deal with a process. Diagrams and maps are also useful for functional language situations (for example, teaching directions).

A more recent genre of image, the 'infographic', blends diagrams, images and words and is more like an 'illustrated text' than an image to support a text. These are beginning to be used in published material as an extension of a reading text or, indeed, as reading texts in themselves.

9. Using other kinds of images: memes

Another recent genre of image, called the meme, is often a combination of an image and text that is humorous in nature and spreads rapidly on the internet. Memes can be used to generate interest in a text (as a lead-in) or like cartoons (matching images and text for humorous results). Students can also be asked to suggest or complete captions for existing memes.

10. A warning about clipart

Clipart is very useful for teaching vocabulary sets or grammar that can easily be represented with pictures. However, many teacher materials suffer from an overuse of bad quality clipart. This is usually the clipart that comes bundled with a word processing program, or that is easily and freely available online. An overuse of cheap clipart makes materials look amateurish. Bear in mind that using a lot of colourful clipart can make material look more appropriate for a younger audience, so it should be used sparingly for material to be used with adults. This isn't to say avoid clipart altogether, but be discerning! There is much more high quality clipart around now than in the past, so it's worth investing some time and energy in finding a good source.

Unit 32

Writing supplementary materials

If you've ever used the teacher's book which accompanies a coursebook, you've probably found and made use of a bank of photocopiable materials at the back. These often include activities like board games or information-gap tasks. These types of activities are frequently used to supplement the core teaching material, providing freer language practice, and often adding a bit more fun to a lesson. Increasingly, these types of materials are also offered online to support courses (now, of course, being termed printable materials rather than photocopiable materials).

Many teachers write their own supplementary materials because, by definition, they want something to 'supplement' their coursebook. However, this doesn't mean that the only use for these materials is to revise or recycle vocabulary in the form of a game or to provide additional speaking practice. With the increasing use of video in the classroom, many teachers now write their own materials to accompany films and short video clips. Progress tests and language reference material also come into the category of supplementary material, and the final unit in this section provides help with writing these.

10 types of supplementary material

Supplementary material refers to extra material that is intended to supplement a coursebook. This usually takes the form of photocopiable material to help support or extend the core material in the student's book. Supplementary material is often the first material that teachers make for their classes on an informal basis, and novice writers who want to get into publishing are often given the task of creating supplementary material to support an existing coursebook before being commissioned to write a full book or course themselves. The good news is that this material is often a lot of fun to create!

Here are 10 types of supplementary material you can write.

1. Board games

There are many variations on traditional board games (eg snakes and ladders) that you can write with a communicative twist. For example, you can create a game where the students have to answer a question or do a task each time they land on a square. For specific ideas and examples of board games, see Unit 34.

2. Dominoes/card games

Cards or dominoes are also relatively easy to create for language learning purposes. They can be used for practising vocabulary, grammar structures or pronunciation. Sets of cards can be made to practise speaking in different situations, or can contain questions which can serve as conversation starters. For specific ideas and examples of dominoes and card games, see Unit 35.

3. Information-gap materials

These are pairwork activities in which Students A and B have material with different information. They have to ask each other questions in order to complete gaps in their information. The material could be two incomplete parts of a travel schedule, different parts of the same story, a map with different parts missing, and so on. See an example on page 83.

4. Questionnaires

While a simple questionnaire can appear on a coursebook page, questionnaires in supplementary material often have more questions, artwork and 'breathing room' (they don't need to be sandwiched in with everything else on a page). Questionnaires work well if all the questions are based on a common theme (or language point) and provoke discussion and exchange of ideas. For more ideas and examples of questionnaires, see Unit 36.

5. Songs

Songs provide a popular form of reading text (the lyrics) and listening text. You'll find 10 ways to use them in Unit 37, but be aware of the copyright issues associated with re-using well-known song lyrics, explained in Unit 47.

6. Videos

Short video clips have always been a favourite area for supplementary materials with teachers and learners. When writing material based on a video, it is common to divide it into three sections: before-watching, while-watching and after-watching. For specific ideas and examples of writing materials for video beyond the basic gap-fill type question, see Unit 38.

7. Online interactive exercises

Materials writers are increasingly writing online support material because many schools have their own online courses. ELT publishers often commission this type of writing nowadays. Writing online exercises often means working with templates and/or specific programs. For more information on the kinds of things you need to know about this type of writing, see Unit 45.

8. Topical lessons

A coursebook is designed to be used at any time of year, with many different kinds of students. As such, it will rarely feature very topical themes or things like local holidays (unless by serendipitous luck). Writing material to coincide with current events or special days is popular with teachers, and publishers often like to have this kind of material online to support existing courses.

9. Flashcards

Of course, writers can make flashcards for almost any age group or level. However, these tend to be more the domain of teaching younger learners. Making flashcards can range from using words and pictures to teach specific items of vocabulary to using images to serve as prompts for more functional language work and role plays.

10. Language worksheets

Perhaps not as glamorous as the other items on this list, the language worksheet is a very common and much-loved type of supplementary material. Teachers sometimes feel that there is just not enough practice of the target language in their coursebook, and want to give their students more. Language worksheets should also have the advantage of allowing more space for the students to write in than is possible in a coursebook. See Unit 25 for ideas and details on writing exercises for this sort of material.

Unit 33

10 tips for creating board games

Board games occupy a special place in materials writing. They can be a lot of fun for the materials writer to make, and they are very popular with teachers and students. Additionally, with modern software it's easy to make simple but good-looking boards. There are a few things you need to know when embarking on creating a language learning board game, though, and it's also useful to see what kinds of games have been produced before. Here are 10 ideas for board games.

1. The basic board

The simplest board for a language learning game is a series of squares going around the page to form a rectangle, with a different task on each square. Make sure your squares are big enough for you to write tasks on them! You can find an example of a board like this on page 170.

2. The snakes and ladders board

Instead of a basic board, this time create a grid of squares. As in the children's game snakes and ladders, include snakes (the head on one square and the end of the tail on another square lower down) and ladders (joining a lower square with a higher square). Then add different tasks to various squares on the board. As in the game above, the students move around the board and do the task they land on. If the player lands at the bottom of a ladder, they go up to the top and do the task. If they land on a snake's head, they go down to the tail and do the task there. You can find an example of a snakes and ladders board on page 172.

3. Dice or no dice

Many traditional board games are designed to be played with dice. This poses two problems for using them in language learning. First, teachers may not always have dice with them in class, or enough dice for all the groups. Second, this means that you need to have far more squares and tasks for the students to do as they may quickly 'pass over' a key square by rolling a five or six. To get around the dice problem, you could design your board game so that the players use a coin to determine how far they move. Heads means move one square, tails means move two squares.

4. Counters

You don't need to make elaborate counters for students to cut out and use in a board game. Students will happily use whatever they have to hand as a counter to move around the board. This might be a ring, a piece of rubber or a small coin. If your board game has squares for players to move through, make sure they are big enough for any one of these unconventional counters.

5. Rules

A good language board game will often have simple rules (eg Throw a coin. Move around the board. Answer the questions). Put these on the actual game board itself, perhaps in the corner or in the middle so that everyone can refer to them as they play. You may have slightly more detailed rules or explanations for the teacher on a separate document.

6. Game-like elements

Once you have your board, and before you add tasks to the squares, you can add various special squares that are typical of board games. These include things like *Miss a turn, Go again, Go forward 2 squares, Pick up a card* (if your board game also has cards), etc. Don't have more than three or four of these, especially on a small board. You want to ensure that the students will land on plenty of language tasks.

7. Board games for vocabulary

For a vocabulary board game, you can put categories or pictures of categories (eg food, drinks, sport, jobs) on various squares. When a student lands on a square, they have to say one or more words in that category. Alternatively, set a mini-challenge on each square for students to answer (eg *Name three things you need to take with you on holiday*). Be careful with questions that have only one possible answer (eg *What is the opposite of happy?*) as this means that that square will only be a challenge for the first person to land on it; subsequent players who land on it will already know the answer.

8. Board games for grammar

Instead of vocabulary questions, a grammar board game will have grammar questions on the squares. Again, try to have questions that might yield many correct answers (for example: Name three irregular past tense verbs) rather than only one. Another option would be to have different categories on the board such as *Correct the sentence, Change the verb tense, Complete the gap* or *Choose the correct answer*. Then for each category, have a list of questions written on a separate worksheet. When a student lands on a square the teacher (or another student) chooses a corresponding question from the category on the worksheet. The advantage of this type of board game is that teachers can customise it by creating their own examples based on grammar they have done in previous classes.

9. Board games for speaking practice

In this type of board game, each square contains a simple speaking task. These could be discussion questions (eg *What do you like doing in your free time?*), instructions to tell a short anecdote or descriptive tasks (eg *Tell us about your last holiday* or *Describe a close family member*), or mini role plays (eg *You are in a clothes shop. Ask for something in a particular size and colour*).

10. Other variations

You can make your board game more interesting by giving the board a theme, such as a town map or a racing track. For a town board game, draw (or find online) a blank map of a town and include various different buildings such as a post office, a train station, a hotel, a souvenir shop, a bank and a police station. For each building, create a list of two or three tasks relating to it. This could be a vocabulary task (*Name three things you can buy in a post office*) or a short role play (*Go to the ticket office and buy a return train ticket to London*). The students move their counters around the town, and when they land on a place, the teacher gives them one of the relevant tasks.

For a racing game, create a board that has several different routes with different starting points. Imagine, for example, a circular race track with four or five lanes or a straight running track with different lanes. Divide the lanes up into squares and assign a challenge for each square. The students then each stay in their own lane and move forwards, or stay put, depending on whether they answer the challenge correctly.

Unit 34

10 other kinds of game to create

There are other kinds of games you can create apart from board games. Card games are also very popular with teachers. There are, in fact, very few language teachers who have not at some point spent time before a lesson cutting out little cards for various activities! Some teachers will also go to great lengths to preserve their favourite language learning card games, laminating the cards and keeping them in special folders. Other common types of games include bingo, word searches and crosswords. The list below includes different kinds of card game and other popular and easy game-like activities you can create to add a play element to classes.

1. Dominoes

Traditional dominoes are sets of small black rectangles, each divided into two, with between one and six spots (as on a dice) at each end. Players have to place them next to each other by matching ends with the same number of spots. For language teaching purposes, instead of spots, dominoes can have words, images, pairs of words with similar sounds, words and possible affixes, etc. – anything that the students can be asked to match. You will need at least 18 pairs of matching items. The best way to make the dominoes is to draw a grid with 36 squares and fill each square with an item from your list of matching pairs. Then cut out the dominoes so that each is made up of two squares. See page 175 for an example of a dominoes game.

2. Pelmanism/Memory game

As with dominoes, you need to produce a list that contains several pairs of matching items to make a pelmanism game work. Create a series of cards, with each card containing one item (word, picture, etc.) from your list. These cards should be big enough for the students to read or identify the object on them easily. To play the game, the students place all the cards face down on the table. They then take turns to turn over two cards at a time, trying to find a match. If they find a match, they keep the cards. If not, they turn them face down again, putting them back in the same place as before. Pelmanism is particularly suitable for the following types of pairs: words and pictures, words and opposites, words and translations, verbs and past tense forms.

3. Happy Families

For this card game, you need to have sets of four cards (a minimum of four sets, or 16 cards). The items in each set must all be in the same 'family'. Ideas for different families could be: groups of semantically linked words (clothes, food, places, jobs), key words and their different forms or words with the same sounds. Each card should have one word on it (perhaps with an image of the word) and the other words in its 'family' written in smaller print at the bottom. The students play in groups of four, taking turns to ask for cards and trying to make their 'family'. See page 176 for an example of a Happy Families game.

4. Story cards

In this game, the students use cards to tell a story. To create the cards, choose an overall theme for the story. This could be a Wild West theme, a Mystery theme, a Fairytale theme, a Sci-fi theme … or a mixture of two or more themes. Put a word and/or picture relating to that theme on each card. The students put the cards face down in a pack. They then tell a story together by taking turns to turn over a card and using the word or picture on their card to continue the story.

Example cards for a Fairytale story theme:

witch, wand, princess, unicorn, castle, dragon, pot of gold, apple

See page 179 for an example of Story cards.

5. What am I doing?

For this game, create a series of cards, each with a sentence describing an action on it (eg *You are drinking very hot tea*). The students take turns picking a card at random (without showing to anyone) and then have to mime the action. See page 180 for an example of a What am I doing? game.

6. Charades

The classic parlour game of charades can be made into a simple card game for the language classroom. Create a series of cards, each with a different word or phrase. In a similar way to the What am I doing? game above, the students have to pick up a card and mime what is on it for the others. For language learning purposes, this can work well with jobs vocabulary, animals or idiomatic expressions (for higher levels).

7. Taboo

Taboo is a definition card game with the twist that you can't use certain words. It is suitable for intermediate and higher levels. For a game of taboo, you need to put a target word on each card and then two or three words that the student is not allowed to use when defining the target word. So, for example, if the target word is *sun*, you might have *hot* and *star* as the taboo words. When the students play the game, they each take a card and try to define the target word without using the taboo words. See page 181 for an example of a Taboo game.

8. Bingo

Everybody loves bingo, and this is an easy game to make. The simplest way is to make a blank 3x3 bingo card and give a copy to each student. Provide a list of at least 25 words that the students have to choose from and tell them to write one word in each square on their cards. Read out the words from the original list at random; the students cross off the words they've chosen when they hear them. The first student to cross off all the words on their card shouts *Bingo!* and is the winner.

Alternatively, you can make all the bingo cards yourself with different words (or pictures) on each one and keep a master set of words to read out.

9. Hidden Treasure

Hidden Treasure is a good game for practising numbers and letters. It's based on the traditional game of Battleships. You'll need to create a 10x10 grid that has the numbers 1 to 10 going across the top and letters A to J going down the left-hand side. The students will use these as coordinates. The students then choose five words. They should have one word with 5 letters, one word with 4 letters, two words with 3 letters and one word with 2 letters. These represent the 'treasures', which they then write in different places on their main grid.

The students then play in pairs, calling out coordinates and trying to 'find' their opponent's treasure. For example, they might call out 'A1' or 'D4'. The opponent says whether this is a 'miss' (the square is blank) or a 'discovery' (there is a letter from one of their words in it). If it is a 'discovery', they acknowledge it is a discovery and say how many letters the word has and what letter has been discovered. That way, the opponent can use their knowledge of language to help them decide whether to call out the square to the left or the square to the right.

Play continues until one student wins by finding the whole of the other student's treasure. See page 182 for an example of a Hidden Treasure game.

10. Wordsearch puzzles and crosswords

Finally, wordsearch and crossword puzzles are very popular with teachers. There are many sites that allow you to make wordsearches and crossword puzzles online (use the term 'word search generator' in a search engine). Wordsearches work well when the students are required to find eight to 10 words from the same lexical set. Crossword puzzles can be made more communicative by filling in half of the answers on one copy of a grid and the other half of the answers on another copy of the same grid. The students then have to define the words in their grid to a partner who has the other half of the puzzle.

"I always try to write classroom games where the students lose themselves in the game and are concentrated on winning on or losing. Language is activated and remembered through generating an emotional response from the learners, like the ones you get when you win or lose a game."

Alastair Lane, teacher, trainer and author, Barcelona

10 variations of questionnaire

Questionnaires generally have a whole set of questions on the same theme and require a personal response. Teachers like them because they can be an effective way of introducing a topic and ensuring lots of genuinely communicative speaking practice with the target language. Students find them engaging because they involve the exchange of real-life personal information and opinions. A well-written questionnaire will have interesting and accessible questions, will generate a lot of speaking and will be user-friendly – in other words, it will be clear what the learners have to do. The following 10 examples show extracts from the beginning of different questionnaires.

1. Straightforward questionnaire to practise a structure

Ask and answer the questions with a partner.

1. Have you ever been to London?

2. Have you ever planted a tree?

3. Have you ever eaten Indian food?

2. Questionnaire based on a set topic or theme

Ask and answer the questions with a partner. Who is more of a film buff?

1. How many films do you watch a month?

2. How often do you go to the cinema?

3. Have you read any books about cinema? Which ones?

3. Find someone who ... questionnaire

Ask questions to other students in the class. When someone answers 'yes', write their name in the space. Find someone who ...

1. likes Sunday mornings _____

2. works at the weekend _____

3. often sleeps after lunch _____

4. goes running in the morning _____

4. Things in common questionnaire or survey

Work in pairs. Ask and answer questions about the topics below. Find things you have in common.

1. Foods I like

2. Foods I dislike

3. Places I've visited on holiday

4. Places I'd like to go

5. Multiple-choice questionnaire

Interview your partner.

1. How often do you walk to school or work? a) never b) once a week c) twice a week or more

2. Do you play sports? a) not since school b) sometimes c) often

3. How often do you take the stairs instead of the lift? a) never if I can help it b) sometimes if it's not too many floors c) whenever I can

Note: This kind of of questionnaire can have a further step where the students count up the choices their partner made and give them feedback (eg mostly answer a = You are not interested in fitness at all!).

6. Student-generated questionnaire

Complete the questions with your own ideas. Then ask the questions to a partner.

1. What's your favourite _____ ?

2. When was the last time you _____ ?

3. When do you usually _____ ?

7. Reverse questionnaire

Look at the answers. Make questions for each answer. Then ask the questions to a partner. Score one point for every answer your partner gives that is the same as on the page.

1. Hardly ever.

2. Once a week.

3. On Friday nights.

8. Opinion questionnaire

Do you agree with these statements? Give each statement a score from 0 (disagree completely) to 5 (agree completely).

Human beings will one day walk on Mars.	*1 2 3 4 5*
Space tourism will happen in my lifetime.	*1 2 3 4 5*
I'd like to travel to space.	*1 2 3 4 5*

9. Importance questionnaires

How important are these things for you in a language classroom? For each question, answer Extremely important, important, somewhat important, not very important or not important.

good lighting

good chairs

a projector and computer

wi-fi connection

10. Star questionnaire

Draw a five-pointed star. At the end of each point, write a name, date or thing that is important to you. Show your star to a partner. Your partner has to guess the questions to give the answers you wrote.

10 ideas for song lesson materials

Song-based lessons are often the first kind of material that a teacher writes. Published materials, while they may contain interesting and varied tasks, will often use recordings of cover versions of older songs. If a teacher wants to work with a current, popular and original version of a song, then they pretty much have to create their own material. It's important, though, to note the complex issues of copyright and permission that surround using song lyrics. See Unit 47 for more detailed information on this area. However, if you have permission from the rights holder to use the lyrics, then here are 10 ideas for song lesson material.

1. Gap fill

The logical starting point for working with a song is simply to gap out key words or phrases. The students can listen and complete the lyrics, or try to complete them first, then listen to the song and check.

2. Put the verses in order

This works well with songs that have three or four different verses and a short chorus, or songs that tell a story. Jumble up the verses. The students try to put the song back in order before listening (if it's a story), then listen and check. Alternatively, they put the verses in order as they listen.

3. Are the words right or wrong?

Make a copy of the lyrics and select a key word every three or four lines. Mark these key words in a different colour or highlight them. Replace some of these key words with other words which would make sense in that spot, and that sound similar. The students listen and decide which of the highlighted words are right and which are wrong. Afterwards, they can read the original lyrics and see what the 'wrong words' should have been.

4. Correct the mistake in the lyrics

Take the song lyrics and rewrite them in certain places slightly differently. The students listen for incorrect words and correct the mistakes. This could also work as an extension to idea 3 above.

5. Use a song as a reading

For songs that tell a story, make a copy of the lyrics and make them into a text that looks more like a prose reading. Write some reading comprehension questions (see Unit 19) and get the students to answer these first before they listen. Play the song at the end.

6. Use a song as a pronunciation exercise

Make a copy of the lyrics and make a gap-fill, taking out pairs of rhyming words (eg *do* and *you*). Jumble these words up and put them in a box at the top of the page. For the first exercise, the students must try to find pairs of words in the box that sound the same. They then listen to you saying the words and they repeat them. After that, they try to put the words back into the right place in the song. Finally, they listen to the song to check.

7. Use a song as a vocabulary exercise

Make a copy of the lyrics and select several key words. Write definitions for these words. Create an exercise that requires the students to find the words in the song that correspond to your definitions. They can do this by listening to the song, or reading the lyrics (depending on how hard it is to make out the words of the song while listening). Alternatively, use images instead of definitions. This activity type is common when using songs with lower levels.

8. Write your own version

Find a song that has lots of examples of 'he said' and 'she said'. Make a copy of the lyrics and gap out some of the parts that come after those phrases. The students then complete the lyrics with their own ideas. Play the song at the end for them to compare with the original lyrics.

9. Cross out the extra word

Make a copy of the lyrics and add an extra word to every third or fourth line. The students first try to identify what they think the extra words are; then they listen and check their answers. Alternatively, they identify the extra words while listening.

10. Include information about the artist and/or the song

Song material can be enhanced by including biographical information about the singer or group (and a picture if possible), or background information about the song or album that the song comes from. This part of the material can form the basis of a before-listening or after-listening activity.

"Students often enjoy translating song lyrics. For the best results, use the songs your students really like."

Magdalena Dygała, teacher and blogger, Poland

10 tips and ideas for writing video lesson materials

Many language classrooms now have projectors and internet availability, giving teachers access to millions of videos of all lengths and genres, from short clips on YouTube to entire feature films. This has led to an enormous growth in the number of lessons in which video plays a part. As a result, there is now increased demand for material to accompany video-based lessons. In many ways, activities written to accompany video material are similar to those written for listening material, but the added visual element gives the materials writer scope for even greater creativity. In the list below, tips 1 and 2 give some general guidelines on writing video-based exercises. Tips 3 to 10 focus on ways of making full use of the images as well as the sound.

1. A three-stage structure

Most video lessons will have the follow stages: a before-you-watch stage, a while-watching stage and an after-you-watch stage. You need at least one activity for each stage, with often a second activity for the while-you-watch stage.

2. Video clips and timings

It's a good idea to break up long videos (anything over three minutes) into smaller clips and have different exercises for each clip. Note that when you need to refer to different times in the video for each activity, add the timings to your rubrics. In other words, a video shown in two parts might have two different exercises with rubrics like this:

- *Watch the first part of the video (0:00 to 1:37) and answer the questions.*

- *Watch the second part of the video (1:38 to 4:05) and answer the questions.*

3. Predict what you will see

A good before-you-watch activity will often involve some kind of prediction. This could be predicting from a series of screenshots (*What do you think the connection between these three images will be?*), from a series of words (*Here are five words that all appear in the video you are going to see. What do you think the video is about?*) or from information about the clips (*You are going to see clips from this summer's blockbuster movies. What movies do you think you will see?*).

4. Tick the things you see

This is a very easy task, suitable for the first while-watching activity. Make a list of eight things (five that appear in the video and three that don't). The students watch and tick the things that appear in the video. If this is key vocabulary, the task can also be used to teach the words. Here is an example of an exercise for a video documentary about a factory process, designed for a technical English course:

Watch the videos and tick the five things you see in the video.

boxes   conveyor belt   shelves   bottles   caps   labels   water   trucks   factory workers

---

5. Put the events in order

As a variation to 4, you could ask the students to watch the video and number the things in the order they see them. This also works well with videos which have a storyline. Prepare a series of statements that describe the events in the video and jumble them up. The students have to number the events in the order they occur. So if you were to show a video from a thriller with a car chase, your exercise might look like this.

Watch part of a film. Number these events from 1 to 5 in the order they happen:

___ The car rolls over twice and catches fire.

___ A police car arrives at the scene of the crime, and two officers get out of it.

___ A man runs down a street and jumps into a car.

___ Two other men suddenly start their engine and follow the first car.

___ A cyclist is knocked off his bicycle into a fruit and vegetable stall.

---

6. Match the quote to the person

Make screenshots of the different speakers in the video and paste them around a piece of paper. Then transcribe one or two lines that each speaker says in the video and write them in the middle of the paper. The students can either watch and try to match the quote to the speaker while watching, or they can watch and try to match the quotes from memory afterwards. A variation would be to put each quote next to the picture of the speaker, but change it slightly so that it has some small errors which the students have to correct while watching.

7. Watch only

For the first while-watching activity, you can prepare a series of questions that the students first try to answer while watching the video with the sound turned off. For more dramatic clips, this could include speculating about what the characters said (especially if this has caused a strong reaction in another character). This is a type of gist-prediction type exercise, so your rubric could be something like this:

Watch the video with the sound off. How do you think the two people feel? What is their relationship to each other?

8. Listen only

This is a reverse approach to the idea in 7. For the first while-watching exercise, the students only hear (but do not see) the video clip. Create a series of gist questions, such as: *Is this a clip from an advertisement, a film or something else? How many people are in this clip? Where do you think they are? What are they doing? What do you think has happened at the end?*

Unit 38

9. Listen and read the script

If you have copies of the script used in the video, you can easily turn it into part of an exercise. For example, you can gap some of the words for the students to listen and complete. One interesting variation on the idea in 8 is to give the students a copy of the script of what the speakers say, but leave space between the lines for them to write what they think they will see on the screen. The rubric could read: *Imagine you are the camera person. Listen to the video and read the script. Write what you think the camera is showing in the video in the spaces in the script.* The next exercise could be: *Now watch the video and compare your ideas with what you can see.* This type of exercise really can draw on a student's visual creativity.

10. Correct the summary

Write a short summary of the video (or a section of it, if it's a long video), including two or three factual errors. The students watch the video or section and identify the errors. A second part of this exercise could involve correcting the mistakes.

If you are working with a long video, the students could then watch the next part of it and write their own summary of this section.

"When creating your own video lesson material, write or record a narration which describes the video but omits essential information (the genre, setting, outcome, etc.). Then, as an exercise, the students hear or read the text before they watch the video and speculate about the missing information."

Jamie Keddie, author of *Videotelling* (videotelling.com)

Unit 38

10 tips on test writing

In earlier units we said that the first kind of material that many teachers write for their classes is a test. Most teachers write their own progress tests because only they know what material they have covered in their classes and what their students can be expected to know.

Good test writers are also very much in demand from publishers. Increasingly, published course materials are accompanied by banks of tests, now mainly online. Writing progress tests is, in many ways, similar to writing practice worksheets. However, there are certain things that you need to keep in mind.

1. Test what you want to test

Make sure that your test questions are testing what they are supposed to be testing. For example, if you are testing knowledge of past tense verbs, your test item should only test that and not require additional skills or knowledge. If your question is supposed to have only one answer, make sure there can, indeed, be no correct answer other than the one you want. Also, when writing progress tests based on what has been taught, make sure your test only tests what you have taught, so that it is fair.

2. Indicate timing

At the beginning of the test, indicate how much time a student has to complete it. If the test has different sections, indicate the amount of time allocated to each part. If the students know how many marks each question has (see 9), they can easily calculate how much time to devote to each set of questions.

3. Start with easier questions before moving to more difficult ones

If an exercise in a test has several items, start with one or two easier items before moving on to the difficult ones. The same applies to question types. Start with easier question types before moving on to more difficult ones. For example, exercises that require the students to choose an option tend to be easier than those that require them to write an answer in a gap. Exercises that require a gap to be filled by a single word or phrase are easier than exercises that require longer pieces of writing.

4. Make sure there is space to answer

Make sure that there is enough space between each line on a test so that the questions can be read easily, and there is room for the students to write their answers. If you have gapped sentences, make sure that each gap is large enough for the answer to be written in. Bear in mind that sometimes a student will write an answer, then cross it out and write another answer next to it. Make your gaps sufficiently large to accommodate this. If a letter or number has to be circled to indicate a correct answer, make sure there is enough space between it and the other choices so there can be no doubt as to which one was chosen.

5. Avoid complicated rubrics

As with writing language exercises, your rubrics for test questions should be very clear. Keep them to one clause, one verb per line. A rubric such as 'Choose the most appropriate tense to complete the gap, using a verb from Exercise 3 above' is far too difficult, whereas 'Complete the gaps using the verbs in the box' is fairly straightforward. For more on rubric writing, see Units 29 and 30.

6. Give an example first

For each question, give a completed example first. This will make the task even clearer. You may wish to include the sentence 'The first one has been done for you as an example' as part of the instructions for a question. Sometimes test-writers include a question numbered zero (0) at the beginning before question (1). This question (0) is completed with the example answer.

7. Check that you have randomised the order of true/false, multiple-choice options

If you include many true/false or multiple-choice questions, check that you have randomised the options and/or order of answers. It is very easy, when writing options, to keep the same order for each one without realising it. Students, however, will notice these patterns as they are doing the test!

8. Discrete and independent items

One thing that makes test writing different from exercises that are designed to 'teach' is that the items on a test should be discrete and independent. This means that if the student gets one wrong, it doesn't mean that they automatically get the rest of the questions wrong as well. So an exercise type which is based on the idea of filling in multiple gaps in a text with a selection of words might not be appropriate; if you get one wrong, you automatically get at least one other one wrong, or if you end up with one word that doesn't fit the last gap, you know you've made a mistake and can go back and try to correct it. Similarly, a reordering exercise where you put a series of sentences in order to make a complete conversation is unsuitable for a test because one mistake will always lead to multiple mistakes.

9. Points and marking

Next to each exercise instruction, indicate the amount of points it is worth. You can do this either by expressing a total (10 points) or by indicating the amount each item is worth and the total points (2 points each, 10 points total). It's handy for marking if you include a line as well for the teacher to write the amount of points scored in the exercise.

At the end of the test, indicate the number of total points and leave a space for the teacher to write the final score. Also bear in mind that you, or another teacher, are going to have to correct dozens (or hundreds) of these tests and give a grade for each one. Make sure your test tallies up to a nice even number like 10 points, 20 points or 100 points. There is nothing more frustrating for teachers and students than to have a test result out of an odd number of points or, worse, out of a very large number of points. Also, if the grades have to be based on a percentage, an even number makes it easy to calculate.

10. Provide the answer key

When you finish writing your test, give yourself a bit of a break, then come back and write the answer key. Even for very simple tests, teachers find it easier to mark if they have an answer key in front of them. Include the point value for each question on the answer key as well.

Writing an answer key also helps you check that your test items work. Sometimes you may find you have written some questions that seemed to have only one answer, but as you write the key you realise there is more than one answer or that it's much more difficult to answer a question than you originally thought. If you have time, it helps to get a colleague to do your test to see that all the questions work.

"When writing questions for a test, I always include one or two easy questions so that everyone gets something right. However, it's also important to include one or two really tricky ones to allow some students to shine."

Alastair Lane, teacher, trainer and author, Barcelona.

Unit 39

10 tips on writing language reference material

Language reference materials, for example the type of reference section you find at the back of many coursebooks, usually include key information about grammar, such as the form, meaning and use. There could also be vocabulary-related materials such as keywords, a pronunciation guide and example sentences. Materials which teach writing skills also tend to include a reference section with model versions of different text genres. Language reference materials don't have to be confined to the back of a book. Many materials, both online and paper-based, are used for self-study, so when the students are completing exercises, they will want to refer to some kind of language reference. This might appear at the click of a button if they are working online, or alongside the exercise in a box if they are working from the printed page.

If you are writing your own materials for use with your students, you might try to include language reference material with any exercises you set for homework. Alternatively, you could create a handout for the students to refer to during the lesson or to take away to use on their own. Such materials are especially helpful for students when they start revising for examinations. Here are 10 tips on how you might approach creating reference materials. Remember that writing this kind of material requires a thorough understanding of every detail related to the language point, so do your homework before writing. It may be worth asking a colleague to check it carefully before giving it to a class. The smallest ambiguity in your explanations could cause problems for the students later on.

1. Tell them

When we write materials for classroom use, we sometimes include tasks where the students discover aspects of the language. This is sometimes referred to as a guided discovery approach and can be used when presenting new items of grammar. However, writing language reference materials is all about telling the students how the language works: the assumption is that the teacher is not there to help and, as a result, there can be no ambiguity. When you write material for the students to refer to, it has to explain the form, meaning and use of the grammar or vocabulary in the simplest, most accessible way.

2. Headings

This is stating the obvious, but write the name of the language point in a bold heading so it's clear what the reference is about. So for a grammar reference, it could be 'Present perfect simple', or for a vocabulary-related reference, the heading could be 'Weather'.

3. Example sentences

It is really helpful to begin by showing the language in context, so present it in a few example sentences. Make sure the sentences don't include vocabulary or other structures that are above the student's current level because the main focus should be on the target language, not on dealing with unknown language in the rest of the sentence. One useful tip is to put the target language in bold or highlight it. Here are some sentences taken from a pre-intermediate level worksheet on prepositions of place. Notice how the other language is right for the level and the target language is in bold:

The book is **on the desk**.

The chair is **next to** the desk.

The desk is **in front of** the window.

4. Pictures and illustrations

In some language reference material, it's helpful to include some kind of visual element. For example, in the previous tip, it might make sense to include a picture of a room with a desk, chair, book and window, appropriately positioned, to accompany the sentences with the prepositions of place. The key point to remember is that any pictures or illustrations with language reference material must be simple and should not require interpretation. The students just need to look and understand, so avoid complex images. Simple free clipart illustrations can often work well. You could even take some photos on your mobile phone: for example, if you need pictures of types of transport, you can walk down any street and take them. They don't have to be great quality for the purposes of language reference.

5. Explaining use

A lot of grammar reference materials include an explanation of how the grammar is used. This can be quite tricky because you have to explain the grammar without using language that is more difficult than the grammar point itself and, therefore, above the students' level. For this reason, you'll need to simplify the grammar explanation for lower levels and sometimes you may feel you are not quite telling the students everything. For example, compare these two extracts from explanations of the present simple at an elementary level and then at an upper-intermediate level:

Use the present simple to talk about routines: I work from 9 to 5 every day.

Use the present simple to talk about habits, routines and regularly repeated events: I sometimes visit my local park./The old man walks past my window every day around six.

Both explanations are presenting a similar use of the present simple, but obviously the second explanation, for the upper-intermediate level, is more sophisticated.

6. Timelines

Sometimes, a timeline can help clarify a form in language reference material. Timelines also help to break up the text on a page and make the reference material more approachable from the point of view of the learner. Here's a timeline contrasting the past simple and past continuous.

They were driving to a party when the car broke down.

7. Form tables

In grammar reference materials, especially for lower levels, form tables are especially useful as they provide a way of summarising how the target language is constructed. If you are preparing information about the form of a tense, you will need to cover the affirmative, negative and question (interrogative) structures in your table, as in this example for how we use the modal verb *can* from elementary level material:

I/You/He/She It/We/They	can can't (cannot)	play the piano.

Can	I/you/he/she/it/we/they	play the piano?

8. Spelling rules

When providing information about changes of word form it's often necessary to include information about spelling rules. Again, putting the spelling changes in bold is an easy way to highlight the area of focus. Here is an example of how you might present some of the spelling rules in a language reference for comparative and superlative adjectives:

- with adjectives ending in -y (after a consonant). change the -y to -i:

  busy → *bus**i**er* - *bus**i**est*

- with adjectives ending in consonant-vowel-consonant, double the final consonant:

  hot → *hot**ter*** → *hot**test***

9. Highlight common mistakes

With some language structures, it can be helpful to highlight mistakes that students often make. When you do this, you must make it very clear what is a sentence with a mistake and what is a correct sentence. For example, if you were writing reference material showing the students how to use modal verbs, you might highlight the fact that the third person form doesn't add -s in the same way that it does with other verbs. In this case, you could write it like this:

He must go to school now. ✔

He ~~musts~~ go to school now. ✘

To make it clear that the second sentence is incorrect, the writer both marks it as incorrect and deletes the error, so it's clear to the students which sentence is wrong and what the mistake is.

10. Consistency

In materials writing, consistency is always important, but for writing language reference materials it is particularly important. Use the same conventions as much as possible so that the students don't have to spend time learning how the references are organised. So if you are writing explanations of use, decide if you will start sentences 'Use the present simple to …', or 'We use the present simple to …', or 'You use the present simple to …' All three

ETpedia: Materials Writing © Pavilion Publishing and Media Ltd and its licensors 2017.

ways of starting your sentences are fine, but try to use the same one every time. Similarly, you could use bold to highlight target language or you could highlight it in different colours; both will work, but try to be consistent throughout. In other words, the students should only need to spend time understanding the content of the language reference materials and not have to deal with inconsistent layouts and formats.

"When writing language reference material, it is important to remember that it is often not possible to give a full explanation of the use of certain language items. Decide what are the most appropriate and useful uses and constructions for the learners you're writing for, and explain these as simply and as clearly as you can. At the same time, make sure that you don't oversimplify and overgeneralise as this could confuse when the learners come across other uses of the language item. Use phrases such as is generally used, is commonly used, can sometimes be used, is used in three basic ways, *and so on to show that other uses are possible."*

Jon Hird, coursebook and grammar book author

Unit 40

Writing materials for other teachers

Throughout this book, we have looked closely at materials designed for use with students in class and for self-study. However, materials writing also includes writing material for the teacher only. In other words, it's the type of writing you find in teacher's books, resource books and methodology titles.

Writing for your fellow teachers requires a different style of writing because the aim is to support and help the teacher – who might also be using in-class and self-study materials you have created. This section provides a checklist of what to include in notes for teachers, as well as suggestions for writing effective teacher resource material. The final unit also gives some tips on sharing your material with other teachers so that your material is starting to 'go public'.

10 features of teacher's notes

Teacher's notes are an instructional guide that might be referred to by teachers from a broad range of backgrounds and with varying degrees of experience: from a novice teacher straight off a training course to a teacher with more than 20 years' experience in the classroom. If you work with a published coursebook, the student's book probably comes with a teacher's book with a complete set of notes for each part of the lesson. Most teacher's books contain the following features, so if you ever need to write a set of notes – even for a short worksheet – that you expect other teachers will use, think about including most or all of the following.

1. Overview of the material

It always helps if there is some kind of short description of what the student's material is about and what the overall aims of the lesson are. This might include reference to the themes of the lesson and the content of the material (especially if it is based on authentic contexts) as well as listing what aspects of grammar or vocabulary will be presented and practised.

2. Answer keys

Most teachers – inexperienced or experienced – refer to the teacher's notes to check the answers. Answer keys save the teacher time and can also be reassuring if an answer is unclear or, perhaps, there is more than one possible answer. The exercise and question numbers in the key should directly match those in the student's book.

3. Listening and video scripts

If the student's material has recordings (audio or video), the teacher will find it useful to be able to refer to transcriptions of these to check anything that the students are having difficulty understanding.

4. Rationale for an exercise

Most teachers will refer to the answer key and the audio/video scripts, but less experienced teachers will also often want a thorough breakdown of how each exercise is going to work. It's often a good idea to state the reason or aim of an exercise using phrases such as: 'This exercise is a lead-in to the topic of …', 'This exercise presents the target vocabulary in the context of …' or 'This role play gives the students the opportunity to practise the language presented in the previous exercise'.

5. Classroom management

If you have explained the rationale of an exercise (see 4), or it is obvious, next you will need to explain how to manage the exercise. For gap-fill type exercises, this should be straightforward: little or no explanation may be needed. However, you might want to make suggestions that relate to classroom management, such as 'The students can work in pairs on this exercise', 'Afterwards, the students can compare their answers in groups' or 'Set a time limit of three minutes for this exercise'. More complex exercises, such as speaking tasks, often require more detailed instructions on how to set up the task, and suggestions for ways to make it more successful.

6. Variations

Certain exercises and tasks in the student's material may be open to variations, depending on the level and ability of the students or the type of class. For example, perhaps a teacher might use the material with a one-to-one class or a class of fifty, in which case you will want to suggest different options. These could appear in the description of how to manage the exercise, or sometimes the teacher's notes can include the sub-heading *Variations* and a paragraph on how to use the material differently.

7. Anticipated problems

As in a lesson plan, it's always helpful for teachers to think about what problems may occur. These might be related to using the material with mixed-ability classes, or perhaps you can predict the types of errors or difficulties that will occur with students at the level the material is designed for. You can never anticipate every problem, but users of the material will appreciate any advance warning you can offer.

8. Feedback and error correction

After some exercises, especially free practice exercises for speaking or writing, include suggestions on how to handle error correction or feedback. Teacher's notes often include ideas such as: 'Monitor the students' conversations and note down any errors. Afterwards, write them on the board and ask the students to say what mistakes they can see' or 'Working in pairs, the students read each other's writing and give peer feedback on the successful use of the target language'.

9. Extra activities and photocopiable activities

Sometimes you might feel the material is going to be too short for a particular teacher's context or that the students will need further practice with a language point. In this case, you might want to offer some suggestions for further activities. The teacher's book can also suggest activities that provide a break from the student's material and offer practice that is more interactive (see also Unit 27, tip 6). The teacher's notes can include a section called *Extra activity* which teachers can do if they have time or can use for review in the next lesson. Many of these extra activities also include photocopiable materials. (See Unit 33 on writing photocopiable materials.)

10. After the lesson

At the end of a series of exercises that form a lesson, the teacher's notes can include ideas for what the students might do for homework to follow up on the work done. This feature could also include suggestions for developing project work or a mini-research task related to the content of the student's material.

Some teacher's notes and teacher's books will also include progress tests based on the student's materials. See Unit 39 on writing tests.

Unit 41

10 tips on writing teacher's notes

When writing teacher's notes to accompany a set of classroom materials (see Units 41 and 42), it's important to remember who you are writing for. With normal classroom materials, you are writing exercises that must be understood both by teachers and students. But with teacher's notes – obviously – you are only writing for the teacher; this requires a quite different style of writing. In one respect, it's easier, because you don't have to adjust the level of the language. However, producing a text that makes something easy to follow requires a different type of writing skill, both in terms of writing style and content. Here are 10 tips that may help you approach writing teacher's notes. You may also wish to refer to the set of teacher's notes which accompanies the example worksheet in the appendix on page 168.

1. Write for the least experienced teacher

Whilst no one wants a set of teacher's notes that is too wordy, as a general rule teachers won't complain if the teacher's notes contain more ideas than they need. They *will* complain if the teacher's notes don't include enough support. So it's wise to assume you are writing for a teacher with little experience. That way, your notes will be useful for that kind of teacher; more experienced teachers can ignore what they already know and jump to the part of the notes that is relevant to them.

2. Numbering

Your teacher's notes should include the same numbering as the classroom materials. So lesson titles, exercise numbers and question numbers, etc. will need to be repeated for ease of reference.

3. Titles and sub-headings

It's important for a teacher to be able to find the information they need in a teacher's book quickly. For example, they might not be interested in an extra activity, but they will want to find an answer key quickly. So as well as including exercise numbers (see tip 2), it's often useful to include sub-headings or text in bold to highlight different sections such as **Audio script** or **Answer key**, or to indicate any additional key features you plan to include such as **Variations** or **Photocopiable activity**.

4. Tone and style

It's important to establish how you will address the reader in your teacher's notes. For example, is the tone to be chatty, informal and friendly? Or do you want it to be direct and to the point? Probably the correct answer is to combine both styles when appropriate. For example, here is an extract from a set of teacher's notes explaining how to start the lesson, using a unit called 'Energy' from a coursebook. The first exercise for the students is to look at a picture and discuss two questions. Notice how the writer switches between an indirect style with full sentences and a more direct style with bullet points.

You might want to start the lesson with the students' books closed.

▶ *Write the title of the unit 'Energy' on the board.*

▶ *Put the students in pairs and give them two minutes to brainstorm different types of energy; eg solar, oil, etc.*

▶ *Write their ideas on the board and help with any pronunciation problems.*

> ▶ *Next, ask the students to turn to the picture on page 20 and look at the image of smoke rising from factories.*
>
> ▶ *Discuss the two questions about the picture as a class.*
>
> *If you have a large class, you could ask the students to discuss the questions in small groups and then summarise their answers to the rest of the class afterwards.*
>
> *Allow about five minutes for this part of the lesson.*

5. Options and suggestions

In the first sentence in the example above, the writer uses a modal verb (*You might want to …*). This is a common technique when you want to offer options to the teacher and suggestions for different ways to approach an exercise. Notice that the penultimate sentence also suggests a way to vary the task with a different type of class (*If you have a large class, you could …*). Again, this is the kind of information that teachers really appreciate in their notes.

6. Direct instructions

As well as offering options (see tip 5), teacher's notes should be direct and to the point. So a lot of teacher's notes use imperative forms and sequencers for the stages of an activity (*Next, ask …, Discuss …,* etc.).

7. Consistency

Once you have established a writing style for your teacher's notes, try to be consistent. If you are using bullet points for instructions, do that throughout. If you use certain systems of numbering and referencing, don't change the format. If you are going to have a special feature called 'Extra activities', make sure it appears regularly, rather than just occasionally.

8. Avoiding repetition of what's in the classroom materials

One common mistake of teacher's notes is that they simply reproduce the rubrics and instructions given in the classroom materials. If the student's book rubric says 'Complete the gaps in this exercise', there is no reason to say the same thing in the teacher's notes. The purpose is to offer support on ways to set up the task or vary it. For example, perhaps the students could do the exercise in pairs, perhaps the teacher could set a time limit, or maybe the students could just complete the exercise orally rather than writing the answers.

9. Extra printables

Sometimes, instead of explaining an extra activity, you'll decide to add a photocopiable page with your teacher's notes. It could be a game-like activity (see Unit 35) which supplements the main material; if so, you'll need to make sure you provide instructions for it and that these are easy to find in the rest of your notes.

Unit 42

10. Provide theoretical background and/or rationale

In recent years, many teacher's books have started to include additional support information on the theory behind the material, the methodology or rationale for the approach. Whilst you might not include all this for a one-page worksheet, it can be helpful for some teachers (see tip 5) if you provide the reason for doing something. In this example from some teacher's notes that accompanied a questionnaire activity designed for use on the first day of the course, the writer explains the reasons for doing it in the first part of the instructions.

As it's the first day of your course, this activity is designed to help the students get to know each other, and to build a sense of community in the class. Students need to realise that everyone else has their own reasons for learning English, and that they should support each other.

Make a copy of the questionnaire for each student. Put them in pairs and get them to take turns to interview each other and write down their partner's answers.

"I always put myself in the teacher's shoes and try to imagine different contexts teachers could be working in. I consider low- and high-tech environments, for example, and try to include activities that will work anywhere."

Nicola Meldrum, teacher's book author, Spain

10 ways to share your materials with other teachers

If you've been making your own materials for students for a while, maybe it's time to take the next step and share your materials with other teachers. There are a number of ways to do this at a local level and at a worldwide level, using the internet.

1. The teacher's room

If you work in a language school, you probably have a room where colleagues meet between classes. This is a good place to share ideas and materials. If you write materials aimed at the same level of students as a colleague is teaching, offer them a copy of the material to use in their class. Get feedback from them and encourage them to share their materials with you. You could also set up a folder on a shelf where teachers can put their own materials for others to use.

2. Send your materials to teaching association newsletters

Teacher organisations such as IATEFL and TESOL publish newsletters for their members, and these often include materials created by teachers. It's a good first step to sharing your work with a much wider audience and, of course, it's very satisfying to see your name in print for the first time.

3. English teaching journals

Magazines for English language teachers such as *English Teaching Professional* and *Modern English Teacher* (see Unit 49 for contact details) invite teachers to send in articles and materials they have written for their students. You also receive a small fee if the material is accepted. The other big advantage is that you'll also get feedback from the magazine's editor, which is very useful.

4. Give a presentation using your materials

If there are local teachers' associations near you, they might be looking for teachers to present their ideas at a workshop. Larger organisations such as IATEFL (www.iatefl.org) hold conferences where you can also apply to give a presentation. When presenting, make use of your materials in your talk or workshop. Other teachers will really appreciate you sharing your ideas and, again, it's a good way to see if your materials work for other people.

5. Publish a blog

Another straightforward way to share your materials would be to set up a blog. Give the site a title and subtitle, and make sure to include the words English language teaching/ELT/materials somewhere in there, or words that refer to the kinds of materials you are publishing (this will make it easier for people using search engines to find them). You can then begin sharing your material by creating new pages or posts. We recommend doing this little by little, and not uploading too much material at the beginning. Build up a following first.

Setting up blogs is quite easy nowadays. We recommend Wordpress, Tumblr or Squarespace to create your site.

Unit 43

6. Set up a Facebook page (not profile)

Less personal than a personal profile, a Facebook page can serve as a simple place for you to share files or links to your material. If you have a blog, post a message on your Facebook page every time you share something new. One of the important differences is that with a page, rather than a profile, you don't have 'friends', only 'likes'. Many stores and companies have Facebook pages. With so many people on Facebook, it's a good way to give teachers a simple way to access to what you've made.

7. Share via other social media

If you're active on other social media, such as Twitter or LinkedIn, you can share materials via those platforms with your followers or colleagues. Note that if you want to increase the number of people looking at your material, you will have to seek out others doing the same thing that you are doing and enter into conversation with them. This could involve commenting on their work, sharing something that someone else has made, or just reaching out and asking for advice. This way you will build your network.

8. Self-publish an ebook

A bigger step is to self-publish an ebook. Amazon is one of the first starting points for self-publishing authors, but there are others as well. Lulu and Smashwords are two sites that provide authors with the tools to create and sell their own ebooks. It's free to create a book at any of these sites and they have detailed guides on how to upload a file to be converted into an ebook.

9. Self-publish a print book

There are several companies that offer print-on-demand services which are useful for self-publishing authors. In the past, you had to order an entire 'print run' of a book, then find a place to store the copies before sending them out to your customers. Now, print-on-demand services mean that when someone wants your book, an individual copy is printed and sent out to them. Making a print book is quite a bit harder than an ebook, though, especially if you do not have any design experience. One of the best-known sites to start print-on-demand is www.createspace.com.

10. Approach a well-known publisher with your material

This is probably the toughest way to get published, and of all the ways to share and publish your materials, it remains the least straightforward. You could send samples of your materials to a mainstream publisher, with a view to having them put into print. However, it's rare that they will want to publish the exact material you have written. Normally, a publisher will have a plan for what they intend to publish and will commission writers to produce materials to fit that plan. Nevertheless, there are cases of teachers being 'discovered' by publishers in this way, and if a publisher sees potential in your material, they might contact you about writing materials such as online worksheets, teacher's books and self-study materials initially. (See also Unit 50.)

Developing your materials writing skills

This final section assumes you have started to write your own materials for your classes and you are interested in taking your skills forwards. It includes ideas for improving your writing skills and the material you produce. It also addresses the fact that you might be writing directly into an online platform or involved in developing digital materials.

If you plan to publish materials in the future, it's also important to become very familiar with the legal issues relating to copyright and re-use of texts and images. The set of 10 questions on this topic in Unit 47 are commonly asked by many materials writers.

Finally, you may well be content writing materials for you, your students and your own language school or institution. But some writers would like to take advantage of the potential that online and self-publishing offers, as well as considering a move into the world of ELT publishing. The final unit in this book suggests some starting points for doing that.

10 ways to edit and improve your materials

As we know from teaching in general, we can always improve our work – and materials are no exception. Once you've written a first draft of some material, there are a number of ways to improve and edit it before you use it or offer it to other teachers to use in their classrooms.

1. Run it through a spellchecker

This is perhaps the most obvious thing, and on many word processing programs you will be doing this anyway. But if you are the kind of person who disables spellchecker because you are writing in different languages or just find it annoying to see words being underlined or autocorrected, turn it back on to check your material. Note the same does not necessarily apply to grammar checking. The nature of materials (with lots of gaps, incomplete sentences, and so on) means that an automated grammar checker has a terrible time figuring out what is real text and what is an exercise.

2. Read it to yourself

This is especially true for dialogues, but it's worth reading through an exercise you've written just to check that it feels right. Doing this sometimes allows you to catch odd turns of phrase, or instructions that don't make as much sense as you thought they would!

3. Write answer keys

Before taking the material into the classroom, it's extremely useful (if not essential) to write an answer key for any exercises. This is a quick and effective way to check if the exercise works and makes sense. Checking and writing answer keys also makes you read the material a second time and highlights any fundamental errors before you give the material to your students.

4. Check your level

When you write materials for different levels, you will start to get a feel for what's 'right' for the level of student you are writing for. But your instincts can only take you so far. There are tools which allow you to check the level of vocabulary you are using in a text. For more information about adapting texts for different levels, see Unit 18.

5. Pilot it

The next thing to do with any exercise or worksheet is to take it into your own class and try it out. Even when you think you have prepared every exercise correctly beforehand, you'll always discover a mistake or some way in which the material could be better. With a whole worksheet containing a series of exercises, you'll sometimes discover that the order of the exercises is wrong or that, in fact, one exercise needs to be removed or a new one added.

6. Pilot it with more than one class

Most teachers know that feeling when you do a lesson again and again and it always seems to be a success. Then one day you use it with a new class, and it fails to engage the students for some reason. That's the reason why it's always worth trying out materials more than once and with different students to gauge how adaptable the material is.

7. Give it to a colleague to pilot

Teaching with your own material is one thing, but giving it to another teacher to use is quite different. When you are working with the material, you can interpret it for the students and adapt it easily because you are familiar with it. Another teacher will have to figure out how each exercise works and deduce the reasoning behind it. That's why teacher's notes are such an important feature of materials writing (see Unit 41). After the lesson, ask the teacher to give you constructive feedback on the material and to talk about how they used it with their students.

8. Ask the students for feedback

As well as asking for feedback from teachers, ask your students what they think of the material as part of a course questionnaire. You don't have to say you wrote the material. Just ask a question like 'How would you rate the materials used in class?' or more specific questions such as 'Is the material just right/hard/easy? Do you find the material useful to refer to after the lesson?'. It's also helpful to know if the topics are of interest and if the students remember what was in the material a few days after the class. Researching this kind of information will give you an idea of whether the material you are writing really 'sticks' with the learners.

9. Develop the design features

Experiment with different ways of presenting your materials because design has a huge impact on how materials are received. Try changing the fonts, colours and the layout of a page. Look at how materials are presented in coursebooks: these are created by experienced ELT designers so you can get ideas from them. However, avoid making your materials too busy or overusing too many colours and fonts: this can make a well-written worksheet unappealing to look at. Again, getting feedback from others on the design should be part of the development process.

10. Go public

Once you've written some material you've piloted, feel proud of and want to share with others, you could look at ways to share it with the wider world (see Unit 43). If you decide to try to publish the material in a journal or teacher's association newsletter, you can get useful feedback from the editor and other readers. If you publish via your own blog or website, people can leave comments on how they've used your material and what worked well about it. (See also Units 49 and 50 for more about publishing your material.)

Unit 44

10 key terms for digital and online materials writing

Whether or not print materials will become obsolete in education is a matter of some debate, but it is undeniable that there is currently more and more digital and online material being created. If you are writing for a publisher, you'll almost certainly be asked to write digital materials at some point. In many ways, almost all the advice given in this book is equally applicable to print and digital material. However, writing for digital has its own special subskills. Moreover, if you are working with publishers or companies in producing digital material, you'll hear a lot of specialist jargon. Here are 10 terms that it is useful for materials writers to know.

1. Template

A template is the structure in which you have to put the content (the actual words of the exercises). Sometimes these are word processing templates, where you are expected to use different styles (a specific font size and format) for different elements of an activity. So, for example, the rubrics are in one style and the exercise sentences are in another style. At other times, the template could be a spreadsheet, and you need to enter parts of exercises into different cells. And sometimes a template is a complete software program in which you have to enter the content into specific boxes. Writing into a template makes the process of turning the content into a digital format easier for the programmers and designers.

2. Flow

In materials writing in general, flow is often used to refer how well (or not) the activities in a lesson or unit work together or connect with each other. Material is said to have flow if the sequence and activities feel right for a classroom. In writing for digital materials, flow is also used to talk about how the content (the exercises and texts) are put into the program. So a developer might say that if the content is put into a template, it can then be flowed into the program.

3. Platform

A learning platform is often compared to an online school or classroom. Basically, it is a online base where various tools or resources can be used by teachers and learners in different ways. A platform is sometimes referred to as a VLE (Virtual Learning Environment) or an LMS (Learning Management System). Examples of different platforms include Moodle, Blackboard and Edmodo. Writers are sometimes asked to write materials for these platforms or, more commonly, for a new platform that a publisher or company might be developing.

4. Drag and drop

One of the most common interactive exercise types, a drag and drop exercise is basically a matching activity where the user must click on an item (a word, phrase or image), drag it and drop it into the correct slot.

5. Iteration

An iteration is a new version of a digital product. Products will often go through various changes before getting launched. These changes continue after they are launched as bugs are fixed in the software and improvements are made, based on user feedback. Each

ETpedia: Materials Writing © Pavilion Publishing and Media Ltd and its licensors 2017.

new version is called an iteration. Some publishers talk about an iterative process for a product, by which they mean that the content will be constantly undergoing changes and improvements during its lifetime.

6. Synchronous and asynchronous

Synchronous online work means that people are working together online at the same time. An online live webinar between a teacher and a class is a synchronous activity. An asynchronous activity means that everybody can do the activity in their own time and they don't all need to be online at the same time. Most material being written for digital is designed to be done asynchronously.

7. Shell

A shell is the name that software developers will give to a program, for example a platform or app, that works but that has little or no content. By making the shell first, they can see what the design looks like and how it works. If you are writing for a digital product, it's helpful to see its shell (also called an initial build) to get a feel for what the material will look like and how it will behave on the screen.

8. Alpha and beta versions

Alpha and beta are terms for software before it is released to the public. The lifecycle of a piece of software traditionally goes through a pre-alpha stage (when it is built), an alpha stage (for initial testing, while the software is not complete) and finally a beta version (where the software is complete, but there may be problems or bugs). Most digital products go through an alpha version and testing with a small group of users, then a beta test with a larger group of users, before getting the final release.

9. Gamification

Gamification refers to the idea of using the features of games in a non-gaming environment. In online materials writing terms, this means that you might add features of online gaming to your materials. For example, perhaps your students get points for getting answers correct and then move up to higher levels the more they get right. Some language learning apps also award badges and prizes to the user once they have achieved a certain score. In the future, if you write online materials, you might find you can add many different features which you would normally associate with computer games.

10. UX and LX

If you are in a meeting with software developers of language learning materials, you might hear them refer to the UX or the LX. These terms mean user experience and learner experience and are often used in reference to the design of the app or website which delivers the learning material. As the writer, you may have little or no control over this experience because it will require the skills of a designer and software developer. On the other hand, if you want to broaden your skillset in the future as a writer, learning about computer coding and how learning apps are created would be advisable.

10 really useful keyboard shortcuts for materials writing

Unit 46

Writing materials can mean sitting in front of a computer for long stretches of time. If you find you're spending time repeating the same tasks over and over again, then keyboard shortcuts are for you. Additionally, if you are a good typist, moving your hands away from the keyboard to fiddle with the mouse on some text can lose you valuable time. Keyboard shortcuts can help here, too. The following keyboard shortcuts can save you time.

1. Select text

Hold down Shift and then press and hold down the arrow keys. This will select the text letter by letter. Holding Shift and Alt together with arrow keys will allow you to select words or lines at a time.

2. Copy

With selected text, press Command + C (Mac), or Ctrl + C (PC). This will copy that text to the clipboard, so that you can paste it in somewhere else.

3. Paste

Press Command + V (Mac), or Ctrl + V (PC) to paste your copied text somewhere else.

4. Undo and Redo

Press Command + Z (Mac), or Ctrl + Z (PC) to undo what you last did. Regret undoing it? Press Command + Y (Mac), or Ctrl + Y (PC) to redo and make things go back to what they were just before you hit undo.

5. Save

Press Command + S (Mac), or Ctrl + S (PC) to save your work. Do this regularly!

6. Overwrite

Select a block of text (see 1) and then just start typing. The new text will appear over it. There is no need to delete the selected text.

7. Find a word or a phrase in a text

Press Command + F (Mac), or Ctrl + F (PC) and type what you are looking for. It should appear highlighted. This is useful for searching webpages for particular words or phrases, too.

8. Quick print

Press Command + P (Mac), or Ctrl + P (PC) to print the document or page that you are currently viewing (this goes to your default printer).

9. Switch between programs or windows

Press Alt + Tab to switch between open programs. So, if you have a word processor and an internet window open, you don't need to move the mouse and click on each one to look at it. Alt + Tab will sort you out.

10. Hyperlink

Select the text you want to link to a webpage, then press Command + K (Mac), or Ctrl + K (PC) to insert a hyperlink. The text should now appear either as purple or blue and underlined. When you click on that text, the linked webpage will open. Note that you can also use hyperlinking to different parts within the same document (you may be doing this if you are working in a template for digital writing).

10 questions on copyright and permissions for materials writers

Throughout this book, we have referred to the fact that teachers use or adapt reading texts, photographs, videos, songs, etc. in their classroom materials. Any teacher and materials writer who chooses to do this needs to be aware of what is or isn't allowed with regard to copyright. Unfortunately, it can be a grey area, and the law may vary from country to country. Here are 10 questions worth asking which will help to guide you in this area.

1. Before you start, can you write it, take it, film it or record it yourself?

Before entering into the area of getting permission to re-use a magazine article or include a photo you've found on the internet, it's probably worth asking yourself whether you could produce something similar yourself. For example, you could perhaps write your own article on a particular topic which contains the target language you need. Similarly, you could take a photograph using your phone or make an audio or video recording yourself. That way, the material is definitely yours to use however you like. Just remember that if you are taking pictures with people in them, you have to be aware of people's privacy; so if you plan on taking a picture of people who could be recognised (especially children) and then sharing and publishing it, it's worth getting their (or their parent or guardian's) signed permission.

2. What is copyright?

Copyright means that the creator of the text, image, video, song, software, etc. keeps control of their creation. So basically, if you want to re-use the content, you may need to approach the owner (who could be the author or the publisher) in order to get permission. One thing worth noting is that anything with copyright is protected until 70 years after the death of the creator. So texts, images, sound recordings and video, whether in hard-copy print or found online, are protected by copyright. Never assume something is copyright-free, even if it doesn't state obviously that it is covered by copyright.

3. Do I need to get permission to re-use part of a written text?

If you plan on quoting from a text which is in copyright, you only have to get permission if you intend to re-use a 'substantial' amount. The problem here is that what is 'substantial' is not well defined in law. Many publishers work on the basis that you can quote up to 50 words from a text and for any number of words over that, you need to get permission. However, with shorter texts such as poems, 'substantial' can mean significantly fewer words. If in doubt, ask for permission from the original author and/or publisher.

4. How do I get permission?

You need to contact the publisher or, if it's something online such as a text, see if it comes with a contact email for the person who created it (the author). You might be asked to pay some money for re-use, but in the case of online content you may find that the person who created it is more than happy to give you permission to re-use their work as long as you credit them. Note that if you want to re-use content from a website, you need to be certain that the website itself had permission in the first place; in other words, it may have re-used content you want from another source.

ETpedia: Materials Writing © Pavilion Publishing and Media Ltd and its licensors 2017.

Unit 47

5. How do I give credit?

The person you need to credit is referred to as the rights holder or the person who gives consent (who is not necessarily the author or creator). If the rights holder allows you to re-use their work, they might tell you what they want the credit line to say about them. At a minimum, a credit should include the author or creator's name, the title and where it came from eg the book or the website. So if you were to quote or re-use content from this book, the credit line would need to say:

Clandfield, L and Hughes, J (2016) *ETpedia Materials Writing* Pavilion

6. What is Creative Commons?

Often when you find content on the internet, you'll see that it comes with a 'Creative Commons' licence. This licence says what you can do with the work you are accessing. So click on the link to see what the Creative Commons licence allows you to do with this particular material. You might also consider applying this kind of licence to your own ELT materials if you decide to put them on your own blog or website for sharing. For more information, visit https://creativecommons.org.

7. Can I re-use an image?

If you want to use a photograph that someone else has taken, all the information in the previous tips applies. See if the photo comes with a Creative Commons license, or contact the photographer and get his/her permission.

Another option is to purchase photos from an image bank such as www.istockphoto.com or http://www.gettyimages.com/. Sites like these have photos for use in publishing. Note that a 'royalty-free' image does not mean that the image can be used free of charge; it means that the image is sold at a flat rate for all purposes. In some cases, you may also need to get consent from the copyright holder of the photo.

Some other sites provide images that are free to use and that specialise in photos with a Creative Commons licence. Sites like Flickr.com and Unsplash.com are two such sites. ELTpics.com is another site, with photos taken by ELT teachers to be used by other teachers in their lessons and materials – as long as you follow the terms of their Creative Commons licence. It's also worth re-stating here the point made in question 1 in this unit. Are you sure you can't just take the photograph you need yourself? That way you own all the copyright to your material.

8. Can I use an online video?

Showing an online video from a site like YouTube in class may or may not be legal. Even if you are showing it for educational purposes and don't intend on making money from it in any way, you need the video-maker's permission (which might be indicated somewhere with the video). In general, videos with adverts or well-known sites like TEDtalks.com are OK to use in your lessons so you can make worksheets to go with them. For more information, the ELT materials writer and video maker Vicki Hollett provides some detail on the legalities of showing videos at http://www.vickihollett.com/can-i-legally-show-this-video-to-my-class/. Again, remember that making your own video content has never been easier, so it might be worth creating your own video instead of using other people's. Note again the issue of people's privacy when filming. (See question 1.)

ETpedia: Materials Writing © Pavilion Publishing and Media Ltd and its licensors 2017.

9. Can I use song lyrics?

Song lyrics are protected by copyright in the same way that any other text is. The music company that represents a musician will control the use of the lyrics and will often charge high permission fees to reprint them in any way. It's for this reason that many mainstream ELT publishers tend to avoid including song lyrics in coursebooks: the permissions process can be expensive, time-consuming and complex.

10. Where can I get more information on copyright and permissions?

Obviously there is much more that could be said on this area, so you might want to do more research. An excellent starting point is the Society of Authors, which publishes a series of free guides for writers, including a 'Guide to copyright and permissions'. Download it for free from http://www.societyofauthors.org/guides-and-articles. It's highly recommended because it covers use of other people's work and it also gives you guidance on how to protect your own materials if you decide to start sharing and publishing them.

"When you film people, even if your stars are your friends, protect yourself by asking them to sign a model release form. This is just a simple document where they say that they agree to let you use their image in your videos for whatever purpose you state in the document. They'll understand, and for you, it's just smart to be safe."

Christina Rebuffet-Broadus, teacher and creator of *Speak Better, Feel Great TV*. Visit her channel at https://www.youtube.com/channel/UCtWyH1MB_A3OggdzoGtkeQA

Unit 47

10 features of a materials writing brief

A writing brief is especially useful if you are planning to write a full set of materials, working with a team of other writers. Typically, major ELT publishers (see Unit 50) develop a brief for all their publications, but a brief is particularly important for any type of materials writing where a number of people are going to be involved in the process. It's also a useful point of reference at planning meetings, and it will be revised over the life of the writing process. If you are writing as part of a team, it's wise to ask for a brief from the person in charge if one isn't supplied. Alternatively, if you are in charge of the project, such as heading a team of teacher-writers creating a set of materials for a course, then write a brief for everyone to follow.

There are no fixed rules when it comes to writing a brief, but it should address the following 10 features and answer the questions given below. You could use the sub-headings given here in your own brief and then write your answers to the questions.

1. The need

What is the main reason for writing the material?

What need does it fulfil that cannot currently be met?

2. Target user

Who will use the materials?

What is the profile of the teacher?

What is the profile of the learner?

3. The level and background of the learner

What is the end-user's level?

What is their learning background?

What are their aims?

4. The approach

What overall methodology or approach will the material follow?

5. The scope of the material

What are the key components of the material? Photocopiable worksheets? Self-study worksheets? CDs? Video? Teacher's notes? etc.

How many lessons need to be produced?

What is the length of a lesson?

How many hours does the material need to cover?

6. Authors

Who are they?

Will the material be co-written or written by individuals?

7. Editorial

Who will oversee and coordinate the materials?

Who will deliver feedback?

Who will ensure deadlines are met?

8. The syllabus

What will the syllabus cover?

What type of syllabus is it?

9. Format and design

What headings and features will be included?

Where will images be sourced from?

Will artwork be needed?

Will there be an external designer?

10. Timing and deadlines

When is the deadline for first drafts?

When is the deadline for receiving feedback?

When is the deadline for second drafts?

When is the deadline for collating and preparing all the materials?

"You can't underestimate the time you need to do your research beforehand ... We spent six months researching our own market and running focus groups with students before any writing began."

John Anderson, British Council project manager with a team of writers developing an online course for Malaysian students

10 ways of developing yourself as a materials writer

Once you've started writing materials, there are many different ways to continue developing as a writer. Writing is much like any other skill; you need to exercise those writing muscles in your brain and in your fingers to get better. Our first and main advice is, therefore, simply to keep writing and trying out your materials with your students and other teachers! However, there are resources and places out there that can help you develop further. Here are 10 suggestions.

1. Find out more about writing professionally

One of the first things to do is to seek out other materials writers who have been doing this for a while. What if you don't know any? Not to worry. A group of ELT writers (including the two authors of this book) have put together a very friendly and accessible guide to the 'industry' of ELT materials writing. It's called *The No-Nonsense Guide to Writing* and contains very useful information about the process of writing, as well as issues such as remuneration, contracts, author promotion and more. It's free to download at http://eltwriters.dudeney.com/.

2. Join a group

You can also become part of a formal group of materials writers in ELT. The two biggest worldwide teaching associations are IATEFL (www.iatefl.org) and TESOL (www.tesol.org). Each of these organisations has a special interest group devoted to materials. For IATEFL it's called MAWSIG and for TESOL it's MWIS. You'll need to be a member of the main organisation to become a member of one of these groups. Both groups have newsletters and hold local and online events. Find out more from the IATEFL and TESOL websites.

3. Consult specialists

ELT Teacher 2 Writer is the name of a group of well-known editors and writers who have put together several useful guides to writing materials from all different areas of ELT. They offer workshops and training as well, and have a database of writers that you can join. This database is frequently consulted by ELT publishers. Find out more at www.eltteacher2writer.co.uk.

4. Write a blog

Many materials writers start spreading their wings online by writing a blog or publishing online. It's easier than ever to do this now, and aside from giving good writing practice, it can often gain you readers and interest when you least expect it. See Unit 43 for tips on how to share your materials online in a variety of ways, including blogs.

5. Develop your keyboard skills

If you are going to spend a lot of time writing, start developing your keyboard skills. Touch typing is an extremely useful skill to have, and it can be learnt (search for 'typing course online' for many examples). You will also want to make things go more quickly by learning keyboard shortcuts. See Unit 46 for a helpful list of 10 of these.

6. Write for publications

We have mentioned before in this book that you can write articles or lesson/activity ideas for different journals in the field. Two of the more practical magazines are *English*

Teaching Professional (www.etprofessional.com) and *Modern English Teacher* (www. modernenglishteacher.com). Both are widely read and have 'Practical ideas' sections that take submissions from readers. Getting something published in one of these magazines is a very good first step to building a writing CV.

7. Self-publish

If you aren't having any luck with publishers, or prefer to write independently but want an audience for your work, another option is self-publishing. It's relatively easy now to self-publish an ebook on Amazon and in other places. The problem with self-published material is that it's of varying quality and it's hard for people to find it. This is where an organisation like The Round comes in. The Round is an independent e-publishing collective in ELT (full disclosure: one of the authors of this book was a founder). The Round takes submissions and helps authors self-publish their books, while ensuring quality and helping them become known. Find out more at their website: www.the-round.com.

8. Read lots of other books

If you are serious about *writing* materials, you should *read* materials. Lots of them. Go to conferences and get sample copies of the kinds of things you eventually want to write. Take things out of your school library. Find free samples of new books at the publisher's websites. Read them and think about what makes them work – or not. Not only will this make you a better writer, it will also give you an idea of what is in the field, what's changing, what's hot and what's not.

9. Join a professional guild

If you do eventually get published, or are doing regular work for a publisher (especially a British one), then think about joining the Society of Authors. This is a great organisation that helps protect the rights of all authors. It gives help with legal advice on contracts and working conditions and has a regular newsletter with information about writing and the book trade. Membership of the Society of Authors also gets you membership with the Authors Licensing and Collection Society (ALCS). The ALCS makes sure writers are paid what's due to them when people use their work, for example through photocopies. Find information about both these organisations at www.alcs.co.uk and www.societyofauthors.org.

10. Professional qualifications

There is no official qualification in ELT materials writing. Most teachers who write materials have taken the required professional teaching qualifications in their country or other internationally recognised teaching qualifications. It goes without saying that to become a well-established published writer probably means you have many years' experience in different types of classroom contexts and you might also observe and train other teachers. This kind of background means you have an awareness of different classroom contexts, which will improve your ability to write materials for use by other teachers. One route to consider is taking an MA in ELT (or equivalent) which includes a component on materials writing or materials development. Note that these courses are by definition academic and analytical: you will spend a lot of time analysing published materials, and only part of the course will involve you creating your own. Nevertheless, it's another route to consider.

Unit 50

For many teachers who move into writing, one route that has been mentioned in this book is to work for a publisher. This could be as an author or, perhaps, as an editor. The following are some of the main publishers in the English-speaking world that specialise in English language teaching materials.

The first four on the list are among the biggest and best-known ELT publishers and publish materials for every area of ELT. However, in recent years the ELT publishing landscape has changed a great deal with the rise of online and digital publishing and so there are many other growing ELT publishers listed below who also commission writers. Some of the smaller publishers tend to specialise in niche areas of ELT such as English for Academic Purposes or teacher resource books and methodology titles. So before you send off your materials, spend some time studying a publisher's website and catalogue to find out what areas of ELT they tend to publish, and think about how your materials might fit into their list. Note that publishers have a high turnover of editorial staff, so the list below does not include individual contact names. If you reach out to a publisher, it's worth asking for the name of a commissioning editor in the department you are interested in.

It's also important to emphasise that the list below is by no means exhaustive. There are many more publishers around the world who specialise in producing ELT materials for schools in their own country or region. For example, in Italy there is ELI publishing or in Poland there is Nowa Era. If you are based in a particular country and have lots of experience of working with and writing for students who share a first language, then approaching this kind of local publisher first could be a very effective strategy.

Note that when approaching any publisher (especially the larger ones) write 'ELT department' or 'ELT division' with the address or look for the ELT pages of their website because their ELT publishing may be only one part of a much larger range of publishing divisions within the whole company.

1 Oxford University Press

Great Clarendon Street
Oxford
OX2 6DP
United Kingdom
http://www.oup.com/elt

2 Pearson Education

Edinburgh Gate
Harlow
Essex CM20 2JE
United Kingdom
https://www.pearsonelt.com

3 Cambridge University Press

University Printing House
Shaftesbury Road
Cambridge
CB2 8BS
United Kingdom
http://www.cambridge.org/elt

4 Macmillan Education

The Macmillan Campus
4 Crinan Street
London
N1 9XW
United Kingdom
http://www.macmillanenglish.com/

5 Cengage Learning

Cheriton House, North Way
Andover
Hampshire
SP10 5BE
United Kingdom
http://www.cengage.co.uk/

7 Helbling Publishing

100 Clements Road
London
SE16 4DG
United Kingdom
http://www.helblinglanguages.com/

9 Richmond Publishing

Richmond
58 St Aldate's
Oxford
OX1 1ST
United Kingdom
http://www.richmondelt.com/

6 Delta Publishing
Quince Cottage

Hoe Lane
Peaslake, Surrey
GU5 9SW
United Kingdom
http://www.deltapublishing.co.uk/

8 Garnet Publishing

8 Southern Court South Street
Reading
RG1 4QS
United Kingdom
http://www.garnetpublishing.co.uk/

10 Collins ELT

Westerhill Road
Bishopsbriggs
Glasgow
G64 2QT
United Kingdom
http://www.collins.co.uk

Unit 50

Pavilion Publishing and Media Ltd

Rayford House
School Road
Hove BN3 5HX
United Kingdom
Tel: 01273 434 943
Fax: 01273 227 308

Visit www.pavpub.com,
www.etprofessional.com or
www.modernenglishteacher.com

"At Pavilion Publishing we welcome ideas for our list of teacher resource books and methodology titles and we've also got two fantastic magazines. We love getting new ideas and articles from people who haven't been published before. Whether you are an experienced writer or a practising teacher with something to say, we would like to hear from you."

Emma Grisewood, Head of ELT, Pavilion Publishing and Media

Appendix

Some of the following resources can be found in colour at:
https://www.myetpedia.com/appendix-materials/

Those that are available are indicated on the page in question.

Unit 5: 10 common grammar points with suggested contexts

1. Present simple: alternatives to the daily routine

The weekly routine (*Every Monday we have a staff meeting*); anniversaries, birthdays or special festive days (*On our anniversary we go to our favourite restaurant*); a morning routine when on holiday (*When he's on holiday he wakes up at 10 and watches TV in bed*); an unusual routine eg of someone who works nights (*She gets home at 5am and sleeps until 12. Then she goes to her yoga class*).

2. Past simple: alternatives to a holiday

A biography of a famous person (*She was born in … she lived in …*); a memorable day in your life such as a wedding or the day a child was born (*It was a sunny day in June. We took a taxi to the hospital …*); an important news event (*We were at school when it happened, we watched on TV …*); retracing your steps to remember something (*OK, I left home at two o'clock and I walked to the shops …*).

3. Present perfect: alternative to questionnaires about experiences

Two friends catching up (*I've finally passed my driving test. What have you been up to?*); someone boasting about themselves, or a relative (*My son has passed all his exams; he's travelled to five countries; he's won lots of medals …*); an interview of a visiting movie star (*Have you visited our city? Have you tried the local speciality?*); a status report on a project (*We've begun the research; we've collected several sample prototypes …*); comparing pictures from different eras of the same place (*They've built a bank on the corner; the park hasn't changed, though …*).

4. Comparatives and superlatives: alternatives to comparing cars

Comparing different capital cities (*bigger, busier, more cosmopolitan, more crowded …*); comparing mobile phones (*smaller screen, bigger memory, faster, more modern …*); comparing houses for rent (*more expensive, closer to public transport, more suitable for families …*); comparing people (*taller, shorter, more outgoing …*).

5. Passive voice: alternatives to cultural quiz

Political facts about a country (*elections are held every four years; education and health are controlled at a local level; laws are voted on in parliament*); discussing art (*was painted by … was made popular in … was sold for …*); describing a process (*the components are mixed together, then put into a large oven …*); before and after photos of a crime scene (*several items were stolen, a window was broken, the police were notified …*); an official apology (*mistakes were made … the situation is being handled … lives were lost*).

6. Second conditional: alternatives to winning the lottery

Thinking about a new job or dream job (*I'd finish work earlier … I wouldn't work on Saturdays …*); discussing ethical dilemmas (*If you were the police officer, would you lie in this situation?*); describing a problem and asking for solutions (*If I were you, I'd tell the truth …*).

7. Modals of obligation: alternatives to signs and notices

Getting ready for a trip (*You should pack lightly … you have to get a visa … you can't take more than one bag on the plane …*).

8. Present continuous: alternatives to describing a scene

Talking about a breaking news story on radio or TV (*Ambulances are arriving on the scene … people are running in all directions … a man is crying …*); talking on a mobile phone (*What are you doing? I'm waiting for the bus … I'm talking on the other line …*); a police stakeout (*The suspect is getting in his car … He's driving up Main Street … He's parking …*); imagining what life is like back home/for a friend on holiday somewhere (*I bet Jane's studying … my parents are going to a concert …*).

9. Reported speech: alternatives to eavesdropping

Sharing office gossip (*Sheila in accounts said six people were going to get fired …*); a news story covering important declarations (*The prime minister said she was happy with the latest results …*); relaying information from a manager/president/chief spy (*OK, the boss said we had to wait here, so we wait here …*).

10. Countable/uncountable nouns: alternatives to describing what is in the fridge

An expedition somewhere exotic (*sunshine, snow, rain, luggage, equipment, tourist information …*); household chores (*laundry, furniture, clothes, rubbish …*).

Unit 21: 10 common functions with suggested contexts

1. **Meeting people (*Hi, how are you? Nice to meet you, etc.*)**

   At a party; at a conference; at a huge family reunion; on the first day of class; at a school reunion.

2. **Giving advice (*You should ... You shouldn't ... It's a good idea to ... etc.*)**

   Discussing things to do in a town with a visitor; talking about places NOT to go and things *not* to do in a town; someone is about to go for a job interview and needs advice; two friends talking about meeting a partner's parents for the first time; talking about the possibility of living abroad.

3. **Making suggestions (*Let's ... Why don't we ...? We could ...*)**

   Talking about things to do at the weekend; suggesting activities for someone's anniversary/birthday; planning a retirement party for a beloved teacher.

4. **Making requests (*Could you ...? Would you mind ...? Can you ...?*)**

   Asking a friend to help you move; you are in hospital and a friend visits (you ask them to do various things for you); a manager assigning the tasks for the day to his/her staff.

5. **Talking about health (*I don't feel well ... I've got a headache ... My back hurts ...*)**

   At the doctor's office; at a pharmacy; to a passer-by after a minor accident; to a lifeguard on the beach.

6. **Asking permission (*Can I ...? May I ...? Is it OK if I ...?*)**

   In a classroom; on the first day in a new workplace; in a shop.

7. **Asking and giving directions (*It's on the left ... Go straight ... Turn right ...*)**

   In a town; in a large building (school, hospital); in a video game; in a car.

8. **Making and responding to offers (*Would you like ...? Do you want ...? Can I help you?*)**

   In a restaurant; giving a VIP a tour of a workplace; at a dinner party; planning a trip.

9. **Going shopping (*How much ...? Would you like a bag ...? Can I try it on? Can I pay by ...?*)**

   In a clothes shop; in a market; in a gift shop; at a garage sale; in a shopping centre.

10. **Inviting and arranging (*Would you like to go out ...? Are you free on ...? I'd love to! Sorry, but I'm busy that day.*)**

    Over the phone; a workplace meeting; inviting someone to a party.

Unit 24: 10 ideas for role plays with sample objectives

1. A party

This could be a celebrity party, a historical party or a theme party (*Star Wars*, Harry Potter, Shakespeare). Role cards have names of celebrities, historical figures or characters within the theme.

Objective: Meet as many people as you can and make small talk. At the end, can you remember who was at the party?

2. Places to live

Half the class are interested in renting or buying a place; the other half are interested in selling or renting out a place. Role cards have either information about what the buyer wants, or what the seller has.

Objective: Find a place you want to rent or buy; rent out or sell your place.

3. News story

Choose or write a short news story. The students have to role-play a follow-up story. Role cards include journalists and characters in the news story.

Objective: Get more details about the news story to create a follow-up interview.

4. At a restaurant

This is one of the most common role plays and role cards usually include waiter and customer. To add variety you could add a manager role card.

Objective: Find out what special dishes of the day are; the manager comes out to see if everything is all right.

5. Art exhibit

The students role-play being artists and critics at a large art exhibit. Role cards are for the critics or the artists. The artists' role cards have a painting/photography/sculpture on them; this is their work of art.

Objective: Explain the significance of your work of art; the critics decide which ones they like best.

6. Dilemmas

Choose an area (eg money problems, love, studying) and generate a series of dilemmas. For example, a money dilemma might be 'You lent a friend some money but don't know how to ask for it back. It's been some time'. The students each get a role card with a different dilemma on it.

Objective: Tell other people your dilemma and ask for advice; at the end, what was the best advice you received?

 Appendix

7. Witnesses

Create a brief description of an event that the police would be called to: a bank robbery, a large demonstration gone wrong, an argument in a night club, a very loud party. Role cards include witnesses, involved parties and the police.

Objective: The police have to figure out what happened and decide who is guilty.

8. Story characters

This can be used any time you finish a story in class. Role cards include characters from the story and journalists.

Objective: The journalists have to interview the story characters about what happened to them.

9. Alien visitor

Aliens have arrived on earth and are being interviewed by government agents. They do not seem dangerous (the aliens) and are curious about our planet. Role cards are for alien or agent.

Objective: Find out as much as you can about each other's planet in the time allowed.

10. Balloon debate

One of the most classic role plays: here the students role-play different characters in a hot air balloon that is going down. Someone has to exit the balloon to keep it afloat. Role cards include names of characters and suggested reasons why they should stay in the balloon. Characters can be real or fictional.

Objective: Decide as a group who has to jump out of the balloon to save the others.

In the city

Vocabulary: Places in the city

1. Do you live in a town or a city? What are your favourite places? What do you do there?

2. Look at these places from a town or city. Match 1–8 to what you do there (a–h).

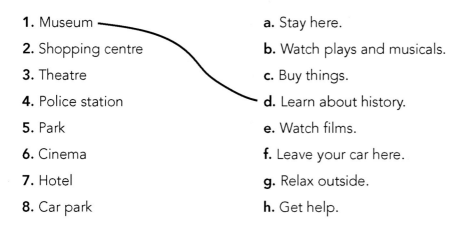

1. Museum

2. Shopping centre

3. Theatre

4. Police station

5. Park

6. Cinema

7. Hotel

8. Car park

a. Stay here.

b. Watch plays and musicals.

c. Buy things.

d. Learn about history.

e. Watch films.

f. Leave your car here.

g. Relax outside.

h. Get help.

3. Look at this map of the city of Oxford. Which places would you like to visit?

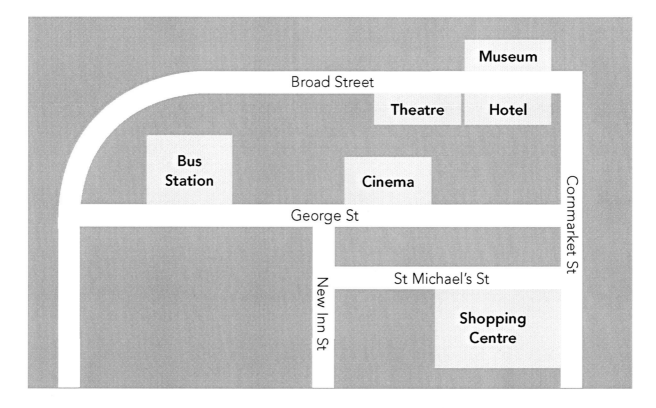

Appendix

Unit 27: Example worksheet

Listening: A conversation in the street

4. **Listen to a conversation. The man is at the bus station. Where does he want to go? Which two streets will he walk along?**

5. **Read the useful phrases. Then write the words in the conversation.**

USEFUL PHRASES: Asking for and giving directions	
Asking for directions	**Giving directions**
Is there … near here?	*It's near here./It's about five minutes away.*
Where's …?	*Go straight ahead/Go straight up this street.*
I'd like to go to …	*Go across the street./Go past …*
	Turn left./Take the first street on the left.
	Turn right./Take the first street on the right.

Man: Excuse me. Is there a shopping centre (1) <u>near</u> <u>here?</u>

Woman: Yes, it's about five minutes (2)_____. Go out of the bus station and turn (3)_____. Go up George Street. Go (4)_____ the cinema and take the first street (5)_____ the right. It's called Cornmarket Street. (6)_____ straight (7)_____ and about halfway down there's a shopping centre on your (8)_____.

6. **Listen and check your answers.**

Speaking: Asking for and giving directions

7. **Work in pairs. Practise similar conversations.**

    Student A: You are at the bus station. Ask for directions to a place on the map.
    Student B: Give Student A directions.
    Now change roles and repeat the conversation.

8. **Ask for and give directions from your classroom to five other places.**

    Example:
    Is there a café near here?
    Yes, there's one about five minutes away. Go straight up …

In the city

Vocabulary: *Places in the city*

1. Discuss these questions together as a class, or put the students in pairs or small groups and have them discuss the questions for two minutes. Then ask them to tell the class their answers. If some of your students don't live in a town or city, they can either describe the place they live or they can choose a town or city they have visited (perhaps the capital city of their country) and comment.

2. Students can work on their own first, and try to match the places, and then check with their partner before checking as a class. For most students at this level, some vocabulary will be familiar (eg *car park*) but some might be new (eg *theatre*).
   Answers: 1d, 2c, 3b, 4h, 5g, 6e, 7a, 8f

   Extension activity

   Put the students in pairs. Student A closes his/her book. Student B has to say definitions of a place in Exercise 2 and Student A has to guess the answer. For example:

   Student B: You learn about history here.

   Student A: A museum.

   Student B: Correct!

3. The students look at the map of Oxford and check that they understand what they can see. For example, ask the class questions such as 'Where can you see plays and musicals?' (Answer: At the theatre). Then encourage the students to say where they would visit if they went to Oxford and to give reasons. By the end of this discussion, the students should be familiar with the location of the places on the map in preparation for the listening task.

Listening: A conversation in the street

4. Play (or read aloud) the following script. The students find the bus station on the map and try to work out where the man wants to go.
   Answer: The man wants to go to the shopping centre. He'll go along George Street and Cornmarket Street.

   Audio script:

   Man: Excuse me. Is there a shopping centre near here?

   Woman: Yes, it's about five minutes away. Go out of the bus station and turn left. Go up George Street. Go past the cinema and take the first street on the right. It's called Cornmarket Street. Go straight ahead and about halfway down there's a shopping centre on your right.

5. Students study the language reference box with the useful phrases. Then they read the conversation and write in the missing words.

6. Play the conversation again and the students check their answers.
    Answers: 2 away, 3 left, 4 past, 5 on, 6 Go, 7 ahead, 8 right

    ### Optional activity

    Before the students start the speaking stage of this lesson, you could drill the phrases in the Useful phrases box for pronunciation practice. Say the phrases and have the students repeat as a class and also repeat individually. Pronunciation of words such as 'straight' and 'ahead' can often cause difficulty for students at this level.

Speaking: Asking for and giving directions

7. Put the students in pairs. They take turns to give each other directions from the bus station to different places on the map. If necessary, do the activity with the whole class by being Student A and asking any student for directions to somewhere.
    As the students practise, listen carefully to their conversations and give feedback afterwards on their use of the phrases.

8. This final activity allows the students to personalise the language for their own location. They take turns to give their partner directions to other places near the classroom. If necessary, think of places near your classroom and write them on the board; for example, *supermarket, local gym, cinema, park etc.* Another option is to show the students a map of the area around your language school so they can refer to it. Either show this on your IWB or projector, or print out copies of the map for the students to use.

    ### Optional task

    If you have a few minutes left or you want to set some homework, ask the students to imagine they are writing an email to a friend who is visiting your home for the first time. In the email, give the friend directions on how to get from the train or bus station to your home.

Unit 34.1: The past and present board game

START / FINISH	WHAT TIME / GO TO BED LAST NIGHT?	WHEN / BE YOUR BIRTHDAY?	GO BACK 1 SPACE
WHERE / LIVE?			WHERE / GO LAST SUMMER?
GO FORWARD 2 SPACES			GO AGAIN
WHAT / DO / LAST NIGHT?			HOW OFTEN / EAT OUT?
WHAT / BE YOUR FAVOURITE TV SHOW?			MISS A TURN
HOW OFTEN / DO EXERCISE?			WHAT / EAT FOR BREAKFAST THIS MORNING?
WHERE / BE BORN?	GO AGAIN	WHAT / DO / LAST WEEKEND?	HOW OFTEN / GO TO THE CINEMA?

THE PAST AND PRESENT GAME

Toss a coin to move around the board.

Heads: Go forward 1 space.

Tails: Go forward 2 spaces.

When you land on a question space, make the correct question and ask a classmate.

When you land on an instructions space, follow the instructions on the space.

You may photocopy this page.

 Appendix

34.1: Blank basic board game for your own use

START			
FINISH			

START / FINISH

You may photocopy this page.

How to play

Toss a coin to move around the board.

Heads: go forward 1 space.

Tails: go forward 2 spaces.

If you land on a ladder, go up the ladder.

If you land on a snake, go down the snake.

If you land on a category, say five words in that category.

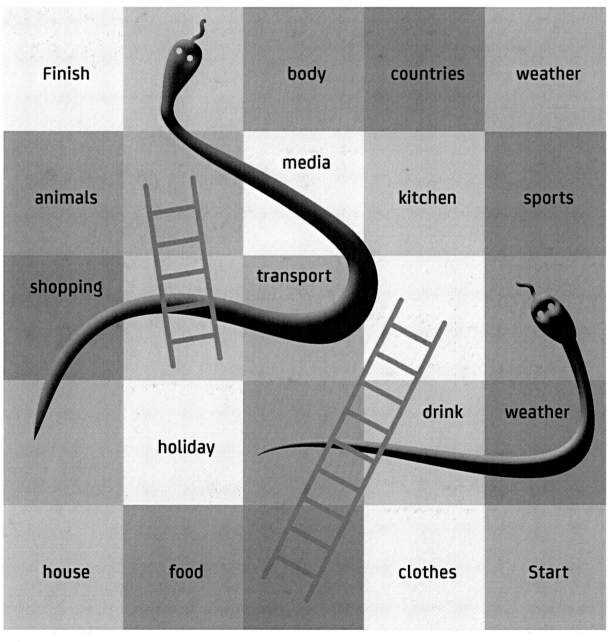

You may photocopy this page.

 Appendix

How to play

Toss a coin to move around the board.

Heads: go forward 1 space.

Tails: go forward 2 spaces.

If you land on a ladder, go up the ladder.

If you land on a snake, go down the snake.

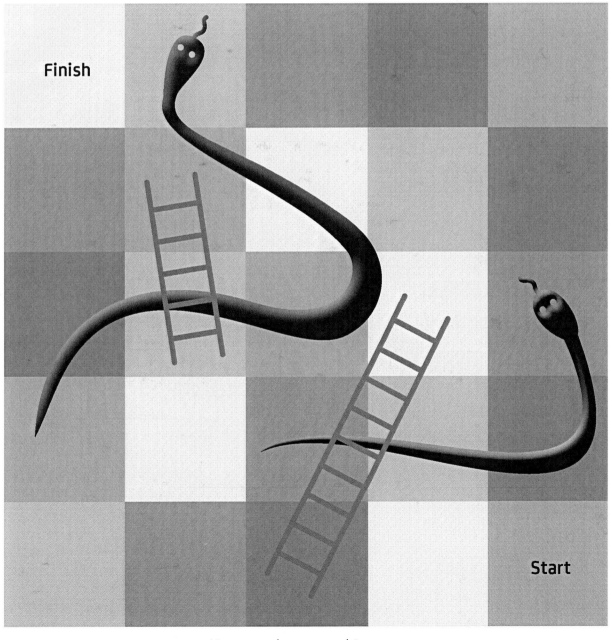

You may photocopy this page.

Blank dominoes for your own use.

You may photocopy this page.

 Appendix

Cut out the dominoes to play.

make	do	strong	have	tell	make	say
goodbye	the price	a nice day	wind	money	the bus	traffic

heavy	be	strong	take	ask	make	say
a question	a look	a word	opinion	thirsty	a joke	housework

do	be	have	deep	take	take	do
hello	trouble	sleep	a mistake	hungry	rain	a photo

heavy	be	have	deep	take	ask	tell
homework	a story	your time	free time	six years old	the bed	yoga

You may photocopy this page.

A full colour version of this material is available at https://www.myetpedia.com/appendix-materials/

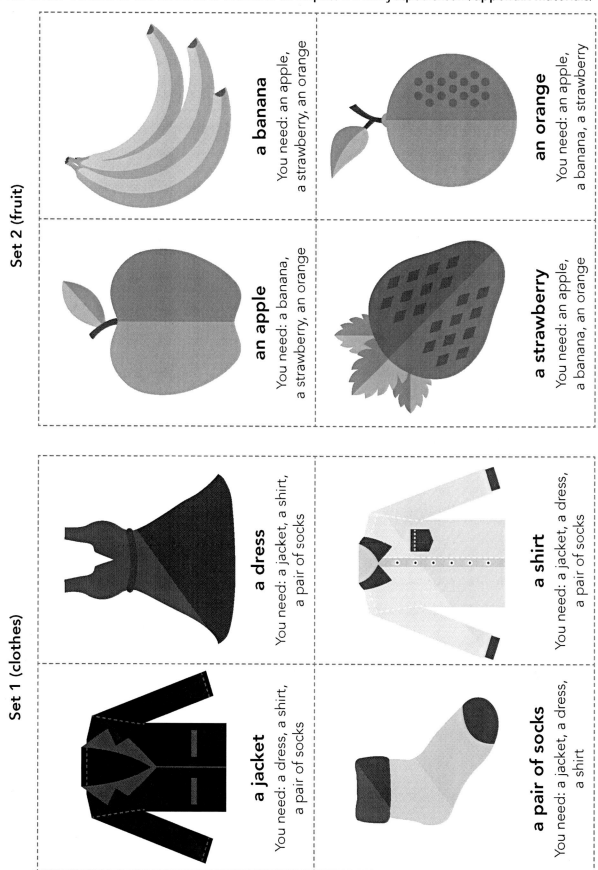

Set 2 (fruit)

a banana
You need: an apple, a strawberry, an orange

an orange
You need: an apple, a banana, a strawberry

an apple
You need: a banana, a strawberry, an orange

a strawberry
You need: an apple, a banana, an orange

Set 1 (clothes)

a dress
You need: a jacket, a shirt, a pair of socks

a shirt
You need: a jacket, a dress, a pair of socks

a jacket
You need: a dress, a shirt, a pair of socks

a pair of socks
You need: a jacket, a dress, a shirt

1. Lexical sets

You may photocopy this page.

 Appendix

Unit 35.3: Happy Families cards

A full colour version of this material is available at https://www.myetpedia.com/appendix-materials/

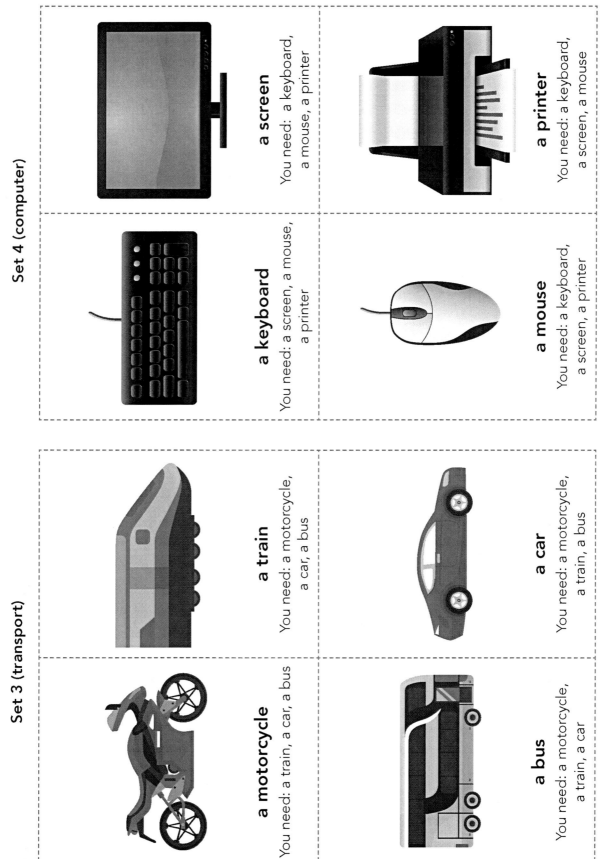

Set 4 (computer)

a screen
You need: a keyboard, a mouse, a printer

a printer
You need: a keyboard, a screen, a mouse

a keyboard
You need: a screen, a mouse, a printer

a mouse
You need: a keyboard, a screen, a printer

Set 3 (transport)

a train
You need: a motorcycle, a car, a bus

a car
You need: a motorcycle, a train, a bus

a motorcycle
You need: a train, a car, a bus

a bus
You need: a motorcycle, a train, a car

1. Lexical sets

You may photocopy this page.

1. Lexical sets

Set 1	Set 2	Set 3	Set 4
use You need: useful, useless, user	**happy** You need: happily, happiness, unhappy	**manage** You need: manager, management, manageable	**succeed** You need: success, successful, unsuccessful
useful You need: use, useless, user	**happily** You need: happy, happiness, unhappy	**manager** You need: manager, management, manageable	**success** You need: succeed, successful, unsuccessful
useless You need: use, useful, user	**happiness** You need: happy, happily, unhappy	**management** You need: manage, manager, manageable	**successful** You need: succeed, success, unsuccessful
user You need: use, useful, useless	**unhappy** You need: happy, happily, happiness	**manageable** You need: manage, manager, management	**unsuccessful** You need: succeed, success, successful

You may photocopy this page.

Appendix

An alien	A spaceship	A scientist
A forest	The moon	A missile
A soldier	A laser gun	An aeroplane
A family	A meteor	

You may photocopy this page.

You are driving a car.	You are eating a plate of pasta.
You are drinking some very hot tea.	You are running and listening to music.
You are watching a scary movie.	You are having an argument on the phone.
You are baking a cake.	You are writing a love letter.

You may photocopy this page.

 Appendix

SUN

yellow

sky

hot

BREAKFAST

morning

eat

food

CAT

animal

dog

pet

GUITAR

instrument

play

music

FOOTBALL

soccer

ball

team

FATHER

mother

parent

family

BED

bedroom

night

sleep

You may photocopy this page.

Unit 35.9: Hidden Treasure

My treasure

	1	2	3	4	5	6	7	8
A								
B								
C								
D								
E								
F								
G								
H								

Think of words for each of your 'treasures'. Then write the word on the My Treasure grid.

Large treasure chest ☐☐☐☐☐☐

Small treasure chest ☐☐☐☐

Jewellery box ☐☐☐

Coin bags ☐☐

Their treasure

	1	2	3	4	5	6	7	8
A								
B								
C								
D								
E								
F								
G								
H								

Large treasure chest ☐☐☐☐☐☐

Small treasure chest ☐☐☐☐

Jewellery box ☐☐☐

Coin bags ☐☐

You may photocopy this page.

 Appendix

Write your own 10 tips

Do you have 10 more ideas for English language teachers? Then why not write them down and share them with your colleagues or share them on the My ETpedia blog at www.myetpedia.com?

1. ....
....
....
....
....

2. ....
....
....
....
....

3. ....
....
....
....
....

4. ....
....
....
....

5. ....
....
....
....
....

Write your
own 10 tips

6. ....
....
....
....
....

7. ....
....
....
....
....

8. ....
....
....
....
....

9. ....
....
....
....
....

10. ....
....
....
....
....

 Appendix